The Rise and Fall of
Corporate New Venture Divisions

Research for Business Decisions, No. 3

Other Titles in This Series

The Rise and Fall
of Corporate New Venture
Divisions

by
Norman D. Fast

umi
RESEARCH PRESS

Library of Congress Cataloging in Publication Data

Fast, Norman, 1948-
    The rise and fall of corporate new venture
divisions.

    (Research for business decisions ; no. 3)
    Bibliography: p.
    Includes index.
    1. Corporations—United States—Case studies. i. Title.
II. Title: New venture divisions. III. Series.

HD2785.F29 1978   658.5'75   78-27096
ISBN 0-8357-0950-7
ISBN 0-8357-0951-5 pbk.

CONTENTS

CONTENTS

APPENDIX

CHAPTER 1

INTRODUCTION

This first chapter is intended to provide the reader with an overview of the objectives of this thesis, the research design and its findings as well as to outline the organization of the chapters that follow.

The Evolution of Corporate New Venture Divisions

The subject of this thesis is a particular approach to the management of new business development in large corporations: the assignment of this task to a separate and often newly created organizational unit which I will call a "New Venture Division."

> *A New Venture Division (or NVD)* is an organizational unit whose primary functions are (1) the investigation of potential new business opportunities, (2) the development of business plans for new ventures, *and* (3) the management of the early commercialization of these ventures.

During the last fifteen years, the NVD approach to new business development has been advocated by several prominent management theorists and consultants.[1] In the wave of diversification which swept through American industry in the 1960's, the NVD's gained widespread popularity. It is estimated that 30 of the 100 largest U.S. industrial companies and as many as 25% of the Fortune 500 adopted this type of structure to facilitate new business development.

A high proportion of the NVD's established during the 1960's and early 70's were short-lived. Of the 18 NVD's studied in this thesis, nine were inoperative by 1976. These had an average life span of only four years. Of the 11 NVD's studied which were established before 1970, seven were inoperative by 1976. They became inoperative either by retaining the ventures they started and growing into an operating division, being assigned a new function - to serve as a staff department, or simply by being disbanded. Several of the surviving NVD's were seen to have evolved as well. Their size, objectives, approach to launching ventures, and the types of ventures they generated were modified and changed through the course of their development. This process of evolution - observed in both NVD's which became inoperative and those which survived - serves as the focus of this thesis.

A Dilemma: The Short Term Life Span of an NVD Versus a Long Term Mission

In contrast to the typically short life span of an NVD, its mission - to start up new businesses - is a long term one. There is substantial evidence that the commercialization of a start-up venture takes a decade or longer. In Harvard Business School doctoral thesis, Eoin Trevelyan found an average of 12 years was required for the commercialization of new ventures while Ralph Biggadike found that eight years was required. In one of the companies studied, Standard Chemicals Company, (disguised name), it was expected that eight years would be required to launch a new venture while at another of the companies focused on (DuPont Company), an internal study found it took an average of 23 years for a new venture to grow to $50 million in sales. The typical short life span of and NVD and this long term mission create an obvious dilemma. A core argument of this thesis is that understanding and managing the evolution of an NVD appears to be one way of resolving this dilemma.

In the section that follows, I will discuss the research design which was followed and the questions which this thesis seeks to answer. In the third section of this chapter, I will briefly summarize my findings. The final section will outline and explain the organization of the chapters which follow.

Research Design and Questions

This research was guided by the following four questions:

   a.   Are there different types of NVD's and in what ways do they differ?
   b.   In what ways do NVD's evolve?
   c.   What factors influence the evolution of an NVD?
   d.   How can the evolution of an NVD be managed?

First Phase of Research

The research design consisted of two phases. The first phase was a broad exploratory survey of 18 companies which had had an NVD at some point during the last decade. Although not a "random" sample, these companies are believed to be representative of the larger population of companies which had NVD's during this period. The primary objectives of this phase of the research were to understand ways in which NVD's differed and their patterns of evolution. A secondary objective was to locate companies for participation in the second phase of the research.

At each of the 18 companies surveyed, the individual who headed up the NVD was interviewed. At several companies, venture managers and staff members were interviewed as well. The time spent at each company varied from one half to a full day.

Discussions with managers at these companies focused on the development of the NVD, the rationale for its establishment, its mission and objectives, its organization and procedures, and characteristics of ventures launched. The conversations were guided by opened ended questions. In most cases, the venture manager provided a chronological recount of the NVD's development and a general overview of how it operated.

Second Phase of Research

The objectives of the second phase of the research were to explore in greater depth the development of several NVD's to understand what factors influenced their evolution and in what ways this could be managed. In-depth case studies of NVD's at three companies were carried out during the first eight months of 1976.

The three companies studied represented different types of NVD's and NVD's which evolved in different ways. At each company, managers at different levels in the organization were interviewed. At least two executive committee members at each company were interviewed to provide a top management perspective of the events that had taken place. At the three companies, a total of nine individuals had headed up the NVD's. Seven of these NVD managers or former NVD managers were interviewed at least once. At each of the companies, several staff members and venture managers within the NVD as well as individuals in the operating divisions were interviewed. In the preparation of the case studies, additional sources of data including memorandums, letters, internal reports, and financial records were utilized.

In both phases of the research, a total of more than 35 days was spent in field research conducting interviews and studying documentation at the companies.

It should be noted that this research is exploratory in nature. Despite the fact that NVD's had been established by a substantial number of major American corporations, there has been a scarcity of research on this particular approach to new business development. The objective of this thesis has been to develop a framework to describe the evolution of NVD's and the factors which influence it. It is not "hypothesis testing" research. Thus, although the findings are strongly supported by the data presented, they are by no means proven. For the sake of style, the tentative nature of the findings is not continually restated.

Summary of Findings

The major findings of this research are summarized below. There are two reasons for doing this. First, it will give the reader an opportunity to decide which parts of this thesis are of interest. If he desires, he can read only the most relevant chapters. Secondly, I believe that the rather lengthy case studies presented in Chapters 4, 5, and 6 will be more meaningful if the reader is given a "map" in advance to focus his attention on particular aspects of the cases.

TYPES OF NVD'S

1.   Two fundamentally different types of NVD's were identified. I have called these a MICRO type NVD and a MACRO type NVD. These differ with respect to their size and objectives, the way in which they develop venture ideas, and the characteristics of the ventures that they launch.

PATTERNS OF NVD EVOLUTION

1.   NVD's evolve in one of two *directions*. They "emerge" - that is they increase in size, importance, and impact on the parent company - or they "decline" in terms of their size, importance, and impact on the parent company.

2.   Five *paths* along which NVD's evolve have been identified. The first two of these are in the direction of "emergence" while the latter three are in the direction of "decline:"

    a.   "Maturing" into an operating division by retaining successful ventures

    b.   Evolving from a MICRO type NVD into MACRO type

    c.   Evolving from a MACRO type NVD into a MICRO type

    d.   Being "redefined" as a staff department

    e.   Being disbanded or "eliminated."

FACTORS DETERMINING NVD EVOLUTION

1.   The major factors influencing whether an NVD "emerges" or "declines" are the parent company's strategic posture (the extent to which it is diversifying or consolidating) and the NVD's political posture (the extent to which its power and credibility and base of support within the parent company is increasing or decreasing).

2.   The specific path of an NVD's evolution is determined by "situational" factors which are identified and discussed in the analysis of each of the three case studies but are not generalizable across companies.

MECHANISMS FOR CONTROLLING NVD EVOLUTION

1.   The ten "mechanisms" listed below can be used by management to control NVD evolution:

      a.   Modifying the NVD Charter
      b.   Modifying the Level of Expectations for the NVD
      c.   Changing the Organizational Positioning of the NVD
      d.   Varying Top Management Support for the NVD
      e.   Selecting the Staff of the NVD
      f.   Specifying Criteria for the Screening of Ventures
      g.   Establishing Integrating Mechanisms for the NVD
      h.   Creating a New NVD
      i   Assigning Additional Functions to the NVD
      j.   Deciding the Timing of Venture Spin-off from the NVD

Organization of Thesis

In the preceding pages, I have briefly described the objectives, research design, and findings of this thesis. Chapter 2 will provide an introduction to corporate new venture divisions. I will discuss the importance of new business development and present evidence that this has been an area of major difficulty for large corporations. The NVD structure has been offered as one approach to this task. The rationale behind an NVD will be discussed and data will be presented indicating the extent to which this approach has been adopted.

Chapter 3 will present the findings of phase one of this research. Two fundamentally different types of NVD's will be described. I will discuss different ways in which NVD's evolve drawing examples from both the three NVD's studies in-depth and the 15 others surveyed.

In Chapters 4, 5, and 6 the case studies of the NVD's of Standard Chemicals, DuPont, and Ralston Purina will be presented. These cases illustrate three different paths of evolution which an NVD can follow. In addition, they focus on different factors influencing that evolution.

1. The DuPont case focuses mainly on the effect of the changing "corporate situation."

2. The Ralston Purina case focuses primarily on the management and impact of the NVD's "political posture."

3. In Standard Chemicals, both the "corporate strategic posture" and the "NVD political posture" were major influences on the NVD's evolution and are focused on in the case.

Chapter 7 will present a framework which incorporates the major factors found to influence the evolution of an NVD. The three case studies will be analyzed and compared with respect to this framework.

Chapter 8 will present the implications for managers and researchers. It will address the question of how the evolution of an NVD can be planned for, managed, and controlled and offer suggestions for future research.

NOTES

[1]See Ansoff and Brandenberg (1971) and Drucker (1974).

CHAPTER 2

NEW VENTURE DIVISIONS: AN INTRODUCTION

This chapter will serve as an introduction to New Venture Divisions. In the first section, I will discuss the importance of new ventures as a topic for research. I will refer to the writings of several prominent management theorists and economists, as well as recent research findings to establish the centrality of new business development to corporate growth and prosperity. Finally, I will offer evidence that large corporations have had difficulty with the management of this activity, and will conclude that new ventures is an important topic for research because it is both significant and problematic.

In the second part of this chapter, I will focus specifically on "new venture divisions." I will discuss the perceived need for NVDs and the rationales which underlie their establishment. I will then report on several surveys indicating the extent to which the NVD concept has gained acceptance in industry.

The Importance of New Ventures

The subject of this thesis combines two of the most important issues facing large corporations today: innovation and diversification.

Innovation

Innovation, "the introduction of new things or methods," is an essential, if not the essential, function of a business organization. In an environment characterized by a rapid pace of economic, social, political and technological change, corporations must be able to respond and adapt effectively if they are to survive.

Joseph Schumpeter, the eminent economist, saw innovation at the heart of our economic system. He wrote:

> "Capitalism . . . is by nature a form or method of economic change, and not only never is, but never can be stationary. . . The fundamental impulse that sets and keeps the capitalist engine in motion comes from the new consumers' goods, the new methods of production or transportation, the new markets, the new forms of industrial organization that the capitalist enterprise creates. . .in capitalist reality, as distinguised from its textbook picture, it is not price competition which counts, but competition which commands a decisive cost or quality advantage, and which strikes not at the

margins of the profits and the outputs of the existing firms but at
the foundations and their very lives.[1]

Peter Drucker has written that because the purpose of a business
is to "create a customer,"[2] innovation and marketing are its basic
functions.

Drucker's emphasis on innovation appears warranted by several
research studies which have shown that innovative companies outperform
their less innovative counterparts. The Department of Commerce Panel
On Invention and Innovation[3] compared the growth rates of four
technologically innovative companies to the rate of increase in Gross
National Product over the two decades from 1945 to 1965. It found that
the four innovative companies increased sales at 16.8% annual rate while
G.N.P. grew by only 2.5% per year.

An M.I.T. researcher compared the performance of four
"innovative" and four "non-innovative" companies over a five year
period.[4] Using the Delphi method, he asked the members of the
Department of Commerce Panel to identify the ten most innovative and
the ten least innovative companies among the 100 largest American
industrial corporations. He found that sales of the four most innovative
companies increased at 16.6% annually, while the four least innovative
companies posted a 6.7% increase. For the innovative companies, profit
as a percent of net worth was approximately 17% compared to about 9%
for the non-innovative companies. The change in stock price showed the
most dramatic difference. The stocks of the innovative companies
increased by more than 110% while the non-innovative stocks declined by
almost 10%.

Diversification

Many business observers also see diversification as essential if a
corporation is to maintain its "fit" with a dynamic environment. Igoι
Ansoff's warning in *Corporate Strategy* is typical:

> "There is considerable evidence to suggest that many firms can no
> longer treat strategic change as a one-time response, put the product-
> market posture in order, and then revert to operating and
> administrative concerns. The post-World War II deluge of
> technology, the dynamism of the worldwide changes in the market
> structure, and the saturation of demand in many major United States
> industries all have contributed to a drastic shortening of the strategy-
> operations-strategy cycle which management used to follow. It
> appears, in fact, that in many industries. . .there is no longer any
> cycle. Strategic change is so rapid that firms must continually survey

the product-market environment in search for diversification opportunities. . . In the present business environment, no firm can consider itself immune to threats of product obsolescence and saturation of demand."[5]

John Glover's research on America's 100 largest industrial companies from 1909 to 1965 has shown dramatically how failure to develop or acquire new businesses in the face of a dynamically changing environment has led to the decline and disappearance of companies and whole industries which were once among America's largest. Figure 2-1 reflects the magnitude of the shifts which took place in little more than half a century:

Figure 2-1
Numbers of Companies by Industry Categories Included in Lists of
100 Largest Industrial and Merchandising Corporations

Industrial Category	1909	1919	1929	1935	1948	1958	1960	1963	1965
Non-ferrous metals	13	12	7	8	7	7	7	5	6
Iron & Steel	11	12	11	10	9	9	9	8	8
"Miscellaneous"	10	2	3	3	3	2	2	2	2
Petroleum	7	19	20	16	18	21	20	18	18
Railroad Equipment	6	4	4	3	2	-	-	-	-
Coal	6	3	4	5	1	-	-	-	-
Food and Beverages	5	6	6	5	5	3	4	4	4
Chemicals	5	5	4	3	8	7	7	8	8
Meat Packing	5	5	2	4	2	2	1	1	2
Agricultural & Industrial Equipment	5	4	1	4	3	4	4	4	4
Shipping and Shipbuilding	4	2	-	-	-	-	-	-	-
Textiles and Leathers	3	2	2	1	2	1	1	1	1
Rubber and Automobile Tires	3	4	4	4	4	4	4	5	5
Lumber, Paper & Paper Products	3	1	3	3	3	4	4	6	5
Tobacco	2	4	4	3	3	3	2	2	2
"Conglomerate"	2	2	2	2	2	4	5	6	6
Electrical Equipment	2	2	2	2	2	2	2	2	2
Distillers	2	-	-	-	3	3	3	2	2
Merchandising & Distribution	1	3	7	9	8	7	7	7	8
Building Materials and Supplies	1	1	2	2	1	-	-	-	-
Communications and Equipment	1	1	2	2	2	3	4	4	4
Containers	1	1	1	2	2	2	2	2	2
Glass	1	-	1	1	2	2	2	2	2
Office Equipment	1	-	-	-	1	1	1	1	1
Automobiles	-	5	4	3	3	3	3	3	3
Motion Pictures	-	-	4	3	4	-	-	-	-
Aircraft, Aerospace & Other Defense	-	-	-	-	-	6	6	7	5
	100	100	100	100	100	100	100	100	100

Source: "Rise and Fall of Corporations: Challenge and Response" by John D. Glover, Harvard Business School Case #PR-6-A (I).

Figure 2-1. Members of Companies by Categories Included in Lists of 100 Largest Industrial and Merchandising Corporations

Glover interprets this data as follows:

As one's eye scans down the list and to the right. . .one gets a 'feel' of *patterns* of change. One is particularly struck most notably by the disappearance from the list of whole industries:-- railroad equipment,

coal, and shipping and shipbuilding.   One notes the scaling-down of
the represenation of other in terms of numbers of companies listed:--
non-ferrous metals and meatpacking, for instance.   In the opposite
direction, one sees powerful movement to the fore in certain other
industries:-- petroleum, merchandising, chemicals, aircraft and
aerospace, and communications and communications equipment.

Some whole groups of companies, it would seem, lost out because
the technologies to which they were wedded, "mature" in Edwardian
times, moved a long way during the half-century from 1909 to 1965
toward obsolescence, at least for certain applications.   They were
involved in industries and technologies that were surpassed by better
ways and means of doing things: The decline of railroad
transportation for passenger travel and for the short-haul of high-
value merchandise obviously affected the rail equipment
manufacturers.   The passing of the use of leather belting in power
transmission and in upholstery had grave impact on leather
companies.   Coal, of course, was displaced by petroleum and natural
gas as sources of energy in important uses.[6]

Glover's research suggests that for many of the single business companies
affected by these rising and falling industry tides, acquiring and
developing new businesses (or failure to do so) had a decisive impact on
their future.

Recent research by Richard Rumelt[7] has shown that
diversification has become a corporate activity of increasing importance
in the last two decades. Rumelt found that the twenty years from 1949
to 1969 witnessed a fundamental strategic and structural change among
the largest companies in American industry. He estimated that in 1949,
30% of the Fortune 500 were diversified, that is, no single product line
accounted for more than 70% of their revenues. By 1969, the percentage
of diversified firms of the Fortune 500 had more than doubled to 65%.
During this period, the percentage of firms with 95% or more of their
revenues from a single product line dropped from 35% in 1949 to 6% in
1969, thus indicating that 94% of the 500 largest industrials had
diversified to some extent by 1969.

Rumelt compared the financial performance of the companies in
his study according to their diversification strategies. He concluded that
companies which had diversified into related businesses outperformed
those which remained in a single business or diversified into unrelated
businesses.

The studies above are consistent in linking new business
development to corporate growth and prosperity. In addition to this
relationship however, there are two additional factors which account for
the importance of new business development:

1. The presence of constraints on the acquisition activity of large corporations

2. The potential benefits of improving return on investments in research and development.

Each of these is discussed below.

Constraints on Acquisition

New venture development and acquisition are alternative vehicles for diversifying. During the late sixties, diversifying acquisition activity, stimulated by high price earnings ratios and popularization of the conglomerate concept, rose dramatically as shown in Figure 2-2.

Figure 2-2
Acquisition Activity—1960-1972

Year	Number of Acquisitions	% Diversifying Acquisitions*	Acquired Assets ($ millions)	% of Assets Acquired in Diversifying Acquisitions*
1960	51	72	1,535	70
1961	46	61	2,003	69
1962	65	67	2,241	54
1963	54	76	2,536	62
1964	73	72	2,303	69
1965	62	73	3,232	83
1966	75	78	3,311	85
1967	138	85	8,259	83
1968	173	87	12,554	90
1969	136	82	10,966	73
1970	90	88	5,876	80
1971	58	91	2,443	80
1972	56	–	1,749	–

*extend operations of firm beyond its present product or geographic markets

Sources: F.T.C. Statistical Report on Mergers and Acquisitions, Bureau of Economics, October 1973, and Markham (1973), pp. 7-11.

Figure 2-2. Acquisition Activity - 1960-1972

As can be seen above, the pace of diversifying acquisitions slowed in the early seventies. This has been attributed to tighter credit, declining price/earnings ratios, more stringent accounting rules, and government anti-trust pressure. It is likely that government anti-trust pressure against acquisitions (including diversifying acquisitions) will remain strong. In the past, upsurges in merger activity have prompted more rigorous enforcement of anti-trust regulations and the passage of new legislation. The Sherman Act, the Clayton Act and the Celler-Kefauver Amendment to the Clayton Act were all enacted during or after major increases in merger activity.[8]

Increase Return on R & D Investment

The second stimulus for interest in new ventures is the desire to realize a greater return from corporate investment in R & D. For several years, there has been an awareness that most companies have reaped only a fraction of the potential harvest from their research laboratories. Almost a decade ago, Ansoff and Stewart wrote:

> Chief executives, who once accepted R & D on faith, are no longer willing to keep hands off and let the technological tail go on wagging the corporate dog. Many are beginning to look for ways to measure results, which they rightly suspect are not always what they should be.[9]

It has been estimated that almost three-quarters of the more than $20 billion annual expenditure on R & D in the U.S. does not yield a profitable product.[10] If the return on investment in R & D is to be improved, much of this improvement will have to take place outside of the laboratory since research typically accounts for less than 10% of the total cost of successful product innovations.[11] The bulk of the funds are consumed in bringing the new product or the new business idea to the market. In other words, improving effectiveness in new business development holds the key to increasing the return on corporate investment in research and development.

Corporate Ineffectiveness in Launching New Ventures

In the discussion above, I have argued that development of new ventures is of great importance to large corporations. Nevertheless, there is substantial evidence that this activity has generally been a stumbling block for many, if not most, large corporations.

The organizational enviroment of a large corporation is generally not conducive to creating, recognizing or commercializing innovative new products. The resistance to innovation which typifies most large companies has often been commented on. Charles Kettering who was responsible for seveal of the most significant innovations in the automobile industry, one stated:

> The greatest obstacle course in the world is trying to get a new idea into a factory.[12]

A study by the consulting firm Booz, Allen, and Hamilton[13] found that organizational problems were cited by more than 80% of the companies surveyed as a major cause of new product failures.

The relative lack of innovativeness of most large corporations has been commented on by the noted economist Richard Caves:

> The large firm with market power may be able to sustain a large scale and extensive development investment. But the small firm often seems more congenial to generating new and truly novel ideas.[14]

Several studies of the sources of innovations and inventions provide supporting evidence for Caves' observation. Although a relatively small number of large companies (those with 5,000 or more employees) account for approximately 85% of expenditures on research and development,[15] independent inventors and small companies have been responsible for a large percentage of the important innovations of this century. Figure 2-3 lists some of these. Additional evidence is provided by the research of Jewkes, Peck, Hamburg and Enos,[16] who found that the majority of important inventions and innovations in several industries and time periods were made by independent inventors or small companies. Even when innovative products or new business ideas with exceptional market potential are brought to the attention of large companies, they are often overlooked. Xerography and Polaroid film are classic examples.

Summary

The studies cited above make clear the importance of new ventures. The writing of Schumpeter, Drucker, Ansoff, Glover and Rumelt have expressed the view that new business development is not only vital to the health of a business enterprise but is essential for a dynamic, growing economy. Government anti-trust activity and

Figure 2-3
Some Important Inventive Contributions of Independent Inventors
and Small Organizations in the Twentieth Century

Xerography 　Chester Carlson	Shrink-proof Knitted Wear 　Richard Walton	Mercury Dry Cell 　Samuel Ruben
DDT 　J. R. Geigy & Co.	Dacron Polyester Fiber "Terylene" 　J. R. Whinfield/J. T. Dickson	Power Steering 　Francis Davis
Insulin 　Frederick Banting	Catalytic Cracking of Petroleum 　Eugene Houdry	Kodachrome 　L. Mannes & L. Godowsky, 　Jr.
Vacuum Tube 　Lee De Forest	Zipper 　Whitcomb Judson/Gideon Sundback	Air Conditioning 　Willis Carrier
Rockets 　Robert Goddard	Automatic Transmissions 　H. F. Hobbs	Polaroid Camera 　Edwin Land
Streptomycin 　Selman Waksman	Gyrocompass 　A. Kaempfe/E. A. Sperry/S. G. 　Brown	Heterodyne Radio 　Reginald Fessenden
Penicillin 　Alexander Fleming	Jet Engine 　Frank Whittle/Hans Von Ohain	Ball-Point Pen 　Ladislao & George Biro
Titanium 　W. J. Kroll	Frequency Modulation Radio 　Edwin Armstrong	Cellophane 　Jacques Brandenberger
Shell Molding 　Johannes Croning	Self-Winding Wristwatch 　John Harwood	Tungsten Carbide 　Karl Schroeter
Cyclotron 　Ernest O. Lawrence	Continuous Hot-Strip Rolling of 　Steel 　John B. Tytus	Bakelite 　Leo Baekeland
Cotton Picker 　John & Mack Rust	Helicopter 　Juan De La Cierva/Heinrich Focke/ 　Igor Sikorsy	Oxygen Steelmaking Process 　C. V. Schwarz/J. Miles

Source: U. S. Department of Commerce, *Technological Innovation: Its Environment and Management*, 1967, p. 18.

Figure 2-3.　Some Important Inventive Contributions of Independent Inventors and Small Organizations in the Twentieth Century

unexploited resources in corporate laboratories make new ventures an activity of paramount importance.　Yet, there is substantial evidence (including the studies by Booz, Allen and Hamilton, the Department of Commerce Panel, Jewkes, Peck, Hamburg, and Enos) to suggest that corporations have had major difficulties in this relatvely unexplored area. It is felt that the significance of new business development and its problematic nature make it a topic worthy of research.

New Venture Divisions:　An Approach to New Business Development

It is generally accepted that the problems large corporations have had with new ventures is due to the fact that tne demands of new business development differ from those of maintaining an existing business.　The belief that a separate organizational unit is required to deal with the demands of new business development has led several of the most well-respected and widely read management theorists to advocate the NVD concept.

Peter Drucker has written:

> The search for innovation needs to be organized separately and outside of the ongoing managerial business. Innovative organizations realize that one can not simultaneously create the new and take care of what one already has. They realize that maintenance of the present business is far too big a task for the people in it to have much time for creating the new, the different business for tomorrow They also realize that taking care of tomorrow is far too big and difficult a task to be diluted with concern for today. Both tasks have to be done. But they are different. Innovative organizations, therefore, put the new into separate organizational components concerned with the creation of the new.[17]

Igor Ansoff, in an article with R. G. Brandenberg has advocated this approach calling it the "innovative form." He explains:

> The underlying principle is to gather currently profitable, established product markets into a current business group and to place development of new product market positions into an innovation group. . . New product market entries are conceived, planned and implemented by the innovation group on a project basis. The group remains responsible for the project until its commercial feasibility has been established. . . At the point of feasibility the project is transferred into the current business group.[18]

Ansoff has recommended this "innovative form" for companies with substantial economies of scale, infexible assets and competences, and long product lives; companies for which it is important to meet the conditions of "steady state efficiency" in their established businesses.

Rationales for NVD Approach

The arguments for establishing NVDs rest on three fundamental principles or rationales:

1. To create a center of responsibility for new business development to assure it receives sufficient attention

2. To provide the organizational climate and structure appropriate for new business development

3. To insulate new business development activities from the dominant values and norms of the parent company.

Center of Responsibility

Creation of a new department to perform a function which has been overlooked or poorly performed by existing departments (in this case new business development) is the traditional bureaucratic remedy for ineffectiveness. March and Simon have explained why the establishment of a separate organizational unit is sometimes necessary. They have found that the propensity of organization members to engage in an activity is a function of the time pressure attached to that activity and the clarity of the goals associated with it. Thus they state:

> We predict that when an individual is faced both with highly programmed and highly unprogammed tasks, the former tends to take precedence over the latter even in the absence of strong overall time pressure. . . If all the resources of an organization are busily employed in carrying on existing programs the process of initiating new programs will be slow and halting at best. Frequently, when a new program is to be developed, a new organizational unit is created and charged with the task first of elaborating the new programs and then carrying on when it has been elaborated.[19]

Discussions with managers involved in new business development confirm that the desire to focus attention on a venture is a basic rationale for separating it from other operations. A typical view was expressed by a corporate executive, who, in evaluating his company's approach toward managing ventures, stated:

> A past mistake has been placing innovative activity under managers whose major responsibility is a traditional activity, and for whom the innovative venture is a minor thing. . . I believe it would be fatal to attach the venture to any one of our other companies. Either the venture will get insufficient nurturing. . .or else the established business will suffer.[20]

Climate and Structure

The second rationale for an NVD is that the organizational climate and structure necessary for "creating" a business are different from those necessary for "maintaining" a business. Burns and Stalker, in their study of industrial firms in the United Kingdom found that different systems of management practices were required by firms operating in a stable environment and those dealing with conditions of change:

> One system, to which we gave the name 'mechanistic,' appeared to be appropriate to an enterprise operating under relatively stable

conditions. The other, 'organic,' appeared to be required for conditions of change.

> In mechanistic systems the problems and tasks facing the concern as a whole are broken down into specialisms. Each individual pursues his task as something distinct from the real tasks of the concern as a whole, as if it were the subject of a subcontract. 'Somebody at the top' is responsible for seeing to its relevance. The technical methods, duties, and powers attached to each functional role are precisely defined. . . Organic systems are adapted to unstable conditions, when problems and requirements for action arise which can not be broken down and distributed among specialist roles within a clearly defined hierarchy. Individual have to perform their special tasks in the light of their knowledge of the tasks of the firm as a whole. Jobs lose much of their formal definition in terms of methods, duties, and powers, which have to be redefined continually by interaction with other participating in the task.[21]

In the language of Burns and Stalker, the NVD serves as an organic enclave within the more mechanistic parent organization. The NVD provides an appropriate sub-system for dealing with the instability and uncertainty inherent in new business development, while the more mechanistic parent organization is suited for the greater stability and certainty in maintaining its existing businesses.

James Hlavacek and Victor Thompson, in an article entitled "Bureaucracy and New Product Innovation" have presented a similar argument in pointing out the need for NVDs to prevent bureaucratic organizations from stifling innovation:

> The bureaucratic strategy has a strong tendency to individualize work and to reduce it in scope and responsibility. By these effects on work, reliability, control, and productivity are all increased, provided there are no counteracting effects. Reliability, control, and productivity, *ceteris paribus*, are also promoted by reducing work to simple repetitive *routines* - by avoiding the insecurities and risks of actual problem solving. Routinization, in turn, depends upon stabilizing the organization's conditions of operation - its markets, products, materials and technology. Far from a drive to innovate, the bureaucratic organization has many reasons for fostering the opposite condition - a tendency to stifle innovations.[22]

Insulate from Values and Norms

The third rationale for an NVD is to free the new business development activities from the dominant values and norms of the parent company. In *Leadership in Administration*, Phil Selznick states that a period of early isolation is necessary for the protection of emerging values and organizational character. He writes:

It follows from our general theory that isolation is necessary during periods of incubation and maturation, but may be modified when this character forming task has been accomplished.[23]

His comments suggest that to new business development often has to be accomplished outside of the existing organization structure:

A new program does not always call for a new organization, but where a new point of view is to be embodied, there is often recourse to a fresh start.   The fear is that the character of the old organization will create resistance to the full development of the new program.   In practical terms, this usually means that the new program, even if accepted in good faith, may be threatened by personnel or budgetary procedures, and by many other operating routines that are uncongenial to it. . . Or, where long established habits of work prevail, a new program may find itself quickly redefined. . .[24]

March and Simon have similarly stated:

. . .It is often said that the creation of a new unit is the only way to secure innovation that is not excessively bound and hampered by tradition and precedent.[25]

A classic example of how attempts at innovation within a corporate environment tend to follow the accepted norms is provided by Ford Motor Company's unsuccessful attempt to design an inexpensive compact car in the late 1930's.   In 1936 Ford set up a task force to develop a low-priced small car.   Working within the existing organization, this task force failed to create the "new" car which was hoped for.   Instead, they designed a scaled down replica of their existing models.   As described by Nevins and Hill:

. . .the 92A, as the car was called, emerged narrower and shorter than the regular Ford, and 600 pounds lighter. . . But difficulties arose.   The small motor cost but $3 less to manufacture than the larger.   The remainder of the car was also cheaper only as it used less material. . .(as the additional saving were only $36) by mid-April the project was abandoned. . .[26]

The need for a separate organizational unit is particularly acute when the venture objectives present a threat to the company's existing business.   It is this rationale which prompted a major oil company to assign its effort to develop an advanced battery for use in an electric car to its NVD, which is organized as a separate subsidiary reporting to the Board of Directors.   Its efforts to develop commercial products in the field of solar energy and development work on a fuel cell, both of which threaten its existing business, are likewise carried out in its NVD.

Summary

Summarizing the discussion above, NVDs have been widely advocated.   The arguments for NVDs rest on three fundamental rationales:

1.   To create a center of responsibility for new business development

2.   To provide an appropriate organizational climate and structure

3.   To insulate new business development from the dominant values and norms of the parent company.

Establishment of NVDs in Industry

The NVD approach to launching new ventures has been adopted by a large number of companies in the last decade. In fact, during the period 1965 - 1970, the NVD concept gained popularity almost to the point of becoming a fad.   Numerous articles appeared in business magazines and journals with titles such as, "Corporate Growth through Venture Management,"[27] "Corporate Venture Groups: Vanguards of Innovation,"[28] "Diversification through Venture Management,"[29] and the like. Newly established NVD were often given widespread publicity and fanfare.

Several studies conducted in the early 1970's provide data on the extent to which NVDs were established. In a 1970 survey, the consulting firm of Towers, Perrin, Foster and Crosby[30] found that at least 27 of the 100 largest U.S. industrial corporations (of the Fortune 500) were practicing venture management.[31]   The companies TPF & C found practicing venture management were spread across several industries as shown in figure 2-4.

In 1972, Kenneth Jones and David Wileman studied venture management in 24 companies.   Extrapolating from their data, they estimated that 25% of the Fortune 500 "now have a venture management operation in one form or another."[32]

A 1973 study by Karl Vesper and Thomas Holmadahl[33] focused on those companies among the top 100 companies which had recently won awards from Industrial Research for introducing significant new products. They found that 65% of these "innovative" companies used venture management and that another 9% planned to use it. Comparing

Industry	Number of Companies
Consumer Products	8
Forestry & Building Products	5
Chemicals	4
Petroleum	4
Information Processing	3
Automotive Products	2
Textiles	1
Aerospace	1
Conglomerate	6
Other	2

Figure 2-4. Distribution of Companies with NVDs by Industry

their findings to the earlier surveys, they concluded that use of venture management was substantially higher among innovative companies.

The surveys cited above suggest that new business development was given high visibility and a great deal of attention by those companies that had established NVDs. Jones and Wileman reported that more than half of the heads of venture groups were appointed to their position by the President or Chairman of their company. Approximately two-thirds sent their reports to the President or Chairman, and in nearly 70% of the companies, go - no go decisions rested with the President or Chairman.

Another measure of the importance of venture activities was their expected contribution to future company sales and profits. In the TPF & C survey, 1970 revenues generated through the venture approach averaged $43 million and were as high as $185 million for one company. Sales from ventures for the 36 companies were projected to total over $7.5 billion by the mid-1970's. In addition, most, if not all companies had projected higher than company return on assets for their ventures.

In their 1973 survey, Vesper and Holmadahl found evidence that interest in venture management was increasing among innovative companies. Approximately one-fourth of the companies which did not have venture groups were planning to establish them. Of companies that had venture groups, 55% planned to increase their budgets while only 6% planned to reduce them. More than half stated that expenditures for initiation of ventures were expected to increase faster than the total R & D budget, while only 11% expected R & D expenditures to increase faster.

To summarize, in the last decade NVD's have gained fairly wide acceptance - having been established by an estimated 25-35% of the 100 largest U.S. industrials. These activities were perceived to be of importance as they reported to top management in most companies and were expected to make an average contribution to sales of over $200 million per company by the mid-1970's.

NOTES

[1]Schumpeter (1950), pp. 82-84.

[2]Drucker (1954), p. 37.

[3]U.S. Department of Commerce (1967), p. 5.

[4]Griffin (1969).

[5]Ansoff (1965), p. 125.

[6]Glover (1967), pp. 17-18.

[7]Rumelt (1974).

[8]See Markham (1973), pp. 2-4 for a more complete discussion of this.

[9]Ansoff and Steward (1967), pp. 71-83.

[10]Hanan (1969), p. 44.

[11]U.S. Department of Commerce (1967), p. 9.

[12]As quoted to in Hill and Hlavacek (1972).

[13]Booz, Allen, and Hamilton (1963).

[14]Caves (1972), pp. 98-99.

[15]U.S. Department of Commerce (1967), p. 9.

[16]The findings of these studies are summarized in U.S. Department of Commerce (1967), p. 17.

[17]Drucker (1974), p. 799.

[18]Ansoff and Brandenberg, (1971), p. 729.

[19]March and Simon (1958), pp. 185-187.

[20]Quotations from managers which appear without footnote are from interviews conducted with managers of NVDs.

[21]Burns and Stalker (1959), pp. 5-6.

[22]Hlavacek and Thompson (1973), pp. 364-369.

[23]Selznick (1957), pp. 126-127.

[24]Ibid.   pp. 41-42.

[25]March and Simon (1958), p. 187.

[26]Nevins and Hill (1962), pp. 117-118.

[27]Hanan, (1969).

[28]Kunstler, (1968).

[29]Oates, (1970).

[30]Towers, Perrin, Forster, and Crosby (1970).

[31]It should be noted the "practicing venture management" does not necessarily mean that an NVD had been established although it is believed that in almost all cases "venture management" fits the definition of an NVD.

[32]Jones and Wileman (1972), p. 15.

[33]Vesper and Holmadahl (1973).

CHAPTER 3

PHASE I: FINDINGS

The two preceding chapters have introduced the reader to corporate NVDs and have presented the research design and organization of the thesis. This chapter will present the findings of Phase I of this research. It will address the two questions listed below:

1. Are there different types of NVDs and in what ways do they differ?

2. How do NVDs evolve?

The discussion of these questions will be presented in three sections. In the first section, I will describe the two fundamentally different types of NVDs which have been identified. These have been labeled the MICRO-NVD and MACRO-NVD.

In the second section, I will discuss the evolution of NVDs. Two aspects of their evolution will be focused on:

1. New Venture Divisions often evolve from the MACRO type to the MICRO type and vice versa.

2. New Venture Divisions tend to become inoperative by evolving in one of three ways which I call "Maturatuion," "Re-definition," and "Elimination."

The chapter will conclude with the identification of a basic dilemma brought about by the patterns of evolution listed above.

In the discussion of types of NVDs and their evolution, several examples drawn from the 18 NVDs studied will be cited. These are offered as "illustrations" to put meat on the skeleton being drawn. The "evidence" supporting the argument presented in this thesis is the case studies presented in Chapters 4, 5, and 6. These are reviewed and analyzed in Chapter 7.

Types of NVDs

By definition, all NVDs are similar in that they (1) investigate potential new business opportunities, (2) develop business plans for new ventures, and (3) manage the early commercialization of these ventures. Nevertheless, significant differences were found among the NVDs in the eighteen companies studied.

Based on the interviews conducted in the first phase of this research, it was observed that two different types of NVDs can be distinguished according to their size and objectives, the way in which new venture ideas are generated and the characteristics of the ventures generated. These two fundamentally different types of NVDs will be called "MACRO" and "MICRO" NVDs.

MACRO and MICRO NVDs are compared below. The descriptions presented are constructs of the researcher and do not portray any particular organization, but rather represent a compilation of characteristics which are usually clustered together. The MACRO and MICRO NVDs represent opposite ends of a spectrum upon which NVDs can be compared. Most NVDs are clearly MACRO or MICRO; however, it should be emphasized that they are not necessarily identical to the "ideal types" described below.

MACRO NVDs

MACRO NVDs, as their name implies, are large new venture divisions often employing several hundred individuals and a budget of several million dollars annually. At their peak, they may be comparable in size to an operating division of the parent company.

They are usually established with a great deal of fanfare and publicity. The NVD has a high profile both within the organization and in the company's public relations. There is an expectation that the NVD will revitalize or redirect the company.

MACRO NVDs often serve as the leading edge of the company's corporation strategy, being given primary responsibility for implementing a diversification program. Thus, their main objective becomes initiating ventures which will make the greatest financial impact on the company, not necessarily those which have the greatest likelihood for success of the highest expected return on investment.[1]

In a MACRO NVD new business ideas are generated within the NVD. Its staff members scan the environment, identify target markets, and formulate new venture ideas. These originate as broadly defined businesses--identified by staff members through their systematic scanning and analysis of the environment. In time they are refined and translated into the specific product concepts. The direction of the idea generating process is from the general to the specific--that is, a broad business concept is refined into specific product ideas. Underlying this process is the assumption that the generation of new business ideas can be rationalized and done systematically.

A MACRO NVD typically launches "frontal assualt" type ventures. These are large scale ventures either aimed at a large segment of a market or consisting of several "parallel" new products aimed at different niches of a broader market. Size is an important criteria in selecting ventures in a MACRO NVD because its primary objective is to have a major impact on the company. The mode of entry is through start-up ventures often in combination with small acquisitions or minority equity investments. The strategy for attacking the target market is to confront it "head on." When problems are encountered, the typical response is to commit additional resources and attempt to solve the problems rather than modifying the strategy of the venture. These ventures are typically aimed at glamorous industries, are characterized by high risk, require a large front end investment, and promise a longterm payoff. Glamorous industries are often sought because of the NVD's high profile and the expectations that have been generated.

The tendency to launch "frontal assault" ventures is attributable in part to the position of the individual who generated the idea. The NVD staff member who initiates the venture in a MACRO NVD is likely to see it in strategic terms--as entry into a broad market. He begins with the legitimacy and access to resources which allow him to launch a "frontal assault." Even when a small venture initiated by a "product champion" is brought into a MACRO NVD, it will often stimulate a formation of a frontal assault around it.

MICRO NVD

A MICRO NVD is a small new venture division established with a low profile and minimal expectations. Often it is intended as a means for retaining internal entrepreneurs, "product champions," and mavericks who do not fit in an operating division or get the support they require there.

A MICRO NVD is not expected to have a major impact on the company. Its role in carrying out corporate strategy is "supplementary"-- that is, it is not expected to bring about a significant redirection of the company. Its mission often includes "trouble shooting" and filling in "gaps" in the corporate strategy--for example, back integrating or introducing a product manufactured by one division into a market served by another division.

Its primary objective is efficiency in new business development-- maximizing the proportion of successful ventures and minizing their cost.

The MICRO NVD serves as a clearinghouse for new business ideas. It evaluates, screens and selects venture ideas which are brought to it and commercializes them.

The sources of new business ideas are dispersed throughout the corporation and external to it. The business idea originates as a specific product. An entrepreneur is the necessary "catalyst" recognizing the potential to couple a specific capability with a specific market need. The direction of the idea generating process is from the specific to the general, that is from a specific product to a broader business concept. Underlying this process is the assumption that new business ideas are generated in a "flash of insight" and cannot be predicted, rationalized or "made to happen" but can only be "captured" when they occur.

A MICRO NVD typically launches "beach head" type ventures. These are small scale start-up ventures built on a single product and aimed at a small well-defined market niche. The strategy for attacking the broader target market is to first to establish a "beach head" in a single niche and then to identify additional market needs and expand outward. This is done by introducing additional products or attacking new niches with the original product.

Ventures launched by MICRO NVDs are characterized by small front end investment and an early break even point. The objective is to test the business idea before making a major commitment. These ventures usually have moderate risk because large commitments are deferred. Because of their small size and low profile, they are very flexible. When major problems are encountered they are often by-passed by a modification of the business idea or change in the venture strategy.

MICRO NVDs tend to launch beach head type ventures partly because of the position of the individual originating the idea. Usually he is a "product champion" and his aim is to sell his invention, not to attack a broader market. The venture idea originates as a specific product designed to fulfill a given market need and the product champion usually does not have the power, resources or inclination to expand his idea into a "frontal assault." His priorities are to develop his product and to penetrate the initial market he sees for it. It is necessary to prove his product to gain support for his venture and this is where his efforts are focused.

Summary

In the section above, two types of fundamentally different NVDs have been identified and described. In the three charts which follow, MACRO and MICRO NVDs are compared. In Figure 3-1, the differentiating characteristics of MACRO and MICRO NVDs which have been discussed above are presented in summary form.

Two MACRO NVDs--Consolidated Paper and U.S. Chemicals (disguised names)--and two MICRO NVDs-- Electronic Corporation of America and Diversified Chemical Company (disguised names)-- are briefly described in Appendix 3-1. These are presented as illustrations of these two types of NVDs. In Figures 3-2 and 3-3, they are compared in

FIGURE 3-1

CHARACTERISTICS OF MACRO AND MICRO NVDs COMPARED

CHARACTERISTIC	MACRO NVD	MICRO NVD
SIZE/OBJECTIVES	• Large scale • High profile and expectations • Objective: to make greatest impact on company	• Small scale • Low profile and expectations • Supplementary role in implementing corporate strategy, often including trouble shooting • Objective: start successful ventures at least cost
IDEA GENERATION	• NVD is venture idea generator • Idea originates as broadly defined business--refined into specific products • Origin of idea: systematic scanning and analysis of environment	• NVD is venture idea clearing house • Idea originates as specific product--develops into broader business concept • Origin of idea: Entrepreneur/inventor/product champion
VENTURES LAUNCHED	• Large scale • Multi-pronged entry including start-up ventures, minority equity investments and/or small acquisitions. • Frontal assault approach • Product line aimed at large market segment • Glamorous, high risk • Large front end investment/long term payoff	• Small scale • Start-up ventures • Beach head approach • Single product aimed at market niche • Moderate risk • Small front end investment/ early breakeven

FIGURE 3-2

MACRO NVDs COMPARED

CHARACTERISTIC	DESCRIPTION OF MACRO NVD	CONSOLIDATED PAPER	U.S. CHEMICALS
SIZE/OBJECTIVES	• Large scale • High profile and expectations • Objective: to make greatest impact on company	• (The NVD) was given the charter to "develop and execute strategies to get Consolidated Paper into new businesses." • "The ventures must be big businesses in order to impact on company profits."	• (The NVD's) charter is "to go into business areas outside of those of the divisions." • The search process is guided by formal corporate objectives • "Our basic criterion is that we want a business with the future possibility of a noticeable impact on earnings per share
IDEA GENERATION	• NVD is venture idea generator • Idea originates as broadly defined business--refined into specific products • Origin of idea: systematic scanning and analysis of environment	• The NVD's functions include the generation of new venture ideas as well as managing their commercialization • There are two venture-generating efforts in the NVD • One group is attempting to identify markets for technological developments • (The other group) has conducted a macro-screen of all the products sold in a supermarket	• New business ideas are generated by a Development Projects department within the NVD. The department ... scans the environment for promising growth areas such as energy and health care • "We are looking for business themes ... then the task remains to translate these into specific product ideas." • Once they have identified target areas, the NVD searches for "leads" or "hints" of technology which the company can incorporate into a venture.

FIGURE 3-2 (Cont'd)

CHARACTERISTIC	DESCRIPTION OF MACRO NVD	CONSOLIDATED PAPER	U.S. CHEMICALS
VENTURES LAUNCHED	• Large scale • Multi-pronged entry including start-up ventures, minority equity investments and/or small acquisitions • Frontal assault approach • Product line aimed at large market segment • Glamorous, high risk • Large front end investment/long term payoff	• Typically ventures launched by the NVD are large • Three of the six ventures launched by the department have had development costs in excess of $10 million • Originally it was planned that they would enter new businesses solely through internal development. Their approach has since broadened to include joint ventures and acquisitions. • The criteria for ventures include size	• Ideally a venture is aimed at a broadly defined market and consists of a portfolio of several individual projects. • "A venture must have a potential of division size-- $100-150 million in sales."

FIGURE 3-3

MICRO NVDs COMPARED

CHARACTERISTICS	DESCRIPTION OF MICRO NVD	ELECTRONICS CORPORATION OF AMERICA	DIVERSIFIED CHEMICAL COMPANY
SIZE/OBJECTIVES	• Small scale • Low profile and expectations • Supplementary role in implementing corporate strategy, often including trouble shooting • Objective: start successful ventures at least cost	• The primary aim of the NVD was to retain internal entrepreneurs. • Four small ventures were launched. They are not expected to have an impact on company earnings.	• Within Diversified Chemical, operating divisions were very active in launching ventures. The NVD's activities accounted for a relatively small part of the company's total new business development efforts.
IDEA GENERATION	• NVD is venture idea clearing house • Idea originates as specific product—develops into broader business concept • Origin of idea: Entrepreneur/inventor/product champion	• The NVD's main functions were described as "selling the concept of the venture program across the company evaluating and screening ideas which were submitted ... and managing the commercialization of the selected ventures." • Most of the internally generated ideas came from the technical and engineering people and middle managers in the company • No ideas which were adopted as ventures were generated at the top of the organization • ...ideas surfaced and were brought to the attention of the NVD	• The functions of the NVD ... are to evaluate select, develop, and commercialize venture ideas that are brought to its attention from within the company • (Company philosophy) stressed the value of the individual. • A large number of new product ideas are generated throughout the organization • "Almost every---employee thinks he can make a new product suggestion ..." • "Project ideas originate at the bottom of the organization most often--that is, at the level of a bench researcher or a salesman

FIGURE 3-3 (Cont'd)

CHARACTERISTICS	DESCRIPTION OF MICRO NVD	ELECTRONICS CORPORATION OF AMERICA	DIVERSIFIED CHEMICAL COMPANY
IDEA GENERATION (continued)		• Three ingredients sought in a venture were a "champion", a unique idea, and a viable business plan • "We were looking for more than a listing of interesting areas like 'we should be in medical electronics.'"	• ... research employees have their own 'pet projects'.
VENTURES LAUNCHED	• Small scale • Start-up ventures • Beach head approach • Single product aimed at market niche • Moderate risk • Small front end investment/early breakeven	• The typical venture was small, capitalized with $200,000.	• "Our philosophy is to give an individual a little to begin with." • There is no minimum size for a venture.

summary form with respect to the characteristics which differentiate
MACRO and MICRO NVDs.

The Evolution of NVDs

NVDs Change Type

NVDs evolve in two ways. First, in terms of the MACRO and
MICRO typology presented above, NVDs change type. MACRO NVDs
may evolve into MICRO NVDs and vice versa. At any point in time,
the majority of NVDs have most of the characteristics of one of these
two ideal types. As an NVD develops however, it sometimes evolves
from one type to the other.

NVDs Tend to Become Inoperative

The second form of evolution is the tendency of NVDs to
become inoperative either by being disbanded or evolving into another
kind of organizational unit.

In most corporations an NVD represents a "paradox" or a
"misfit." It is neither a staff department nor an operating division--but a
hybrid of the two. Because of this peculiar identity, it exists in a state of
disequilibrium. It tends to have a relatively short lifespan (approximately
four to five years) and to become inoperative by evolving in one of the
following three ways:

> Maturation - the NVD indefinitely retains ventures that it launches
> and matures into an operating division
>
> Elimination - the NVD is disbanded
>
> Redefinition -   the NVD is redefined as a staff department.

Each of these is discussed below.

Maturation

The function of an NVD is to create new business. However,
rather than retaining them and growing with them as an operating
division would do, it must divest them and begin the process anew. If
an NVD does not divest itself of successful ventures, its primary function
shifts from the initiation of new businesses to the management of existing
businesses. This is the process of "maturation." When it is complete,
the department ceases to be an NVD.

Redefinition

In the process of redefinition the NVD is transformed into a staff department. Its function usually becomes limited to developing business plans for new ventures which are then turned over to the operating divisions for commercialization. However, this new function may also include corporate planning, environmental scanning, market research, acquisitions, or other functions for which the NVD personnel appear to be well suited. As with maturation, redefinition is usually a gradual process involving the scaling down of personnel and budget and the spin-off of ventures at an early point in their development. When redefinition occurs, the department ceases to exist as an NVD as it no longer is responsible for managing the early commercialization of ventures.

Elimination

Elimination is the third way that NVDs become inoperative. In the process of elimination, the NVD is disbanded as a department. This may occur as a gradual process with elimination being the culmination of a reduction in staffing and budget for the NVD, or it may be abrupt with the department being disbanded by management decree.

Emergence and Decline

Five different paths of evolution that an NVD can follow have been described. These are:

1. Evolving toward a MACRO NVD

2. Evolving toward a MICRO NVD

3. Evolving toward maturation

4. Evolving toward redefinition

5. Evolving toward elimination

Evolving toward a MACRO NVD and maturation are similar in that both represent the "emergence" of the NVD. That is, the NVD increases in terms of the size of its budget and staff, its significance, and its potential impact on the company.

Evolving toward a MICRO NVD, redefinition and elimination reflect the "decline" of an NVD. Its budget and staff decrease as does its significance and potential impact on the company. The various paths of "emergence" and "decline" of an NVD are shown in figure 3-4.

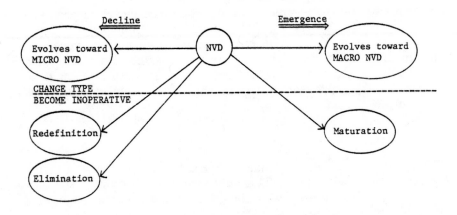

Figure 3-4. Emergence And Decline of an NVD

A Dilemma: The Long Term Mission versus The Short Life Span of NVDs

The first phase of this research exposed a fundamental dilemma regarding NVDs: they have a long term mission but typically have a short life span.

Long Term Mission

The mission of an NVD--to start up new businesses-is a long term one. Just how long a process new business development is, is unclear. To some extent this is because of the lack of a definite beginning and a definite end. Ian Trevelyan, in a Harvard Business School doctoral thesis,[2] estimated that it took approximately twelve years to launch a new venture. At DuPont Company, an internal study found that it took 23 years on the average before a new business reached $50 million in sales. At Standard Chemical Company [3] it was hoped that ventures would break even in five years, but after some experience this was subsequently lengthened to eight years. The average time for new products to break even at Standard Chemical was believed to be about seven years. At other companies studied, the commercialization of a start-up venture was expected to take six to ten years and sometimes longer. Although one of the purposes of a new venture division was to speed this process, there was little evidence that progress had been made in this respect. Thus, it could be said with little controversy that more than five years is required to launch a new venture.

Short Life Span

In contract, NVDs typically have a short life span--an average of four to five years for those which have become inoperative.

The tables below present data on the life-span of 18 NVDs for which this information was obtained. These NVDs were selected from a list of approximately 25 companies known to have had NVDs during the Sixties or early Seventies. Since it is not randomly selected, this sample may not be representative of the population of NVDs in large American companies.[4] The detailed data from which these tables were compiled is presented in Appendix 3-2:

As can be seen in Figure 3-5, in exactly half of the companies for which data was collected, the NVD had become inoperative by 1975. The distribution of this data by the year in which the NVD was established is significant. Seven of the ten NVDs established between 1960 and 1969 were inoperative by 1975. As shown in Figure 3-6, the average life span of the seven which became inoperative was 4.7 years. Of NVDs started after 1970, two had already become inoperative by 1975, surviving only one and two years. The five surviving NVDs averaged only two and a half years in age and it appeared that at least one of these would become inoperative by the end of 1976.

The Dilemma

The nature of this dilemma should be apparent. If NVDs are to be successful at their mission, a means of insuring their long term survival must be discovered. This will require an understanding of why they evolve in the way they do--that is, what factors influence their evolution?--and how their evolution can be controlled--in what ways can the evolution of NVDs be managed? These two questions will serve as the focus for the chapters which follow.

THE LIFE SPANS OF NVDs

	TOTAL	BREAKDOWN BY YEAR NVD ESTABLISHED		
		Before 1960	1960–1969	1970–1975
Total Companies with NVDs	18	1	10	7
NVDs Surviving in 1975	9	1	3	5
NVDs Inoperative in 1975	9	0	7	2

Figure 3-5

AVERAGE AGE/LIFE-SPAN

	TOTAL	BREAKDOWN BY YEAR NVD ESTABLISHED	
		1960–1969	1970–1975
NVDs Inoperative in 1975 (Average life-span)	4.0 years	4.7 years	1.5 years

Figure 3-6

NOTES

[1] It should be noted that a successful venture may have little impact on a company while an unsuccessful venture sometimes has a major impact (i.e., bringing about re-examination of corporate strategy, developing skills and capabilities which will play an important future role).

[2] Trevelyan (1974).

[3] Disguised name.

[4] The list of companies with NVDs was compiled from a variety of sources including annual reports, articles on venture management, researchers, consultants and managers in the field. The companies included in the sample are those in which the NVD manager was successfully contacted and provided the requested information.

CHAPTER 4

STANDARD CHEMICAL COMPANY NEW VENTURE DIVISION

Evolution from 1968 to 1976

The New Venture Division at Standard Chemical was established in 1968. At that time, the company had sales of more than $700,000,000 and a net income of approximately $50,000,000. Sales had increased each of the prior ten years and profits were the second highest in the company's history.

Standard Chemicals diversified product line consisted mainly of products from three raw materials: nitrogen, cellulose, and petroleum. Although research was begun on utilization of a fourth raw material in the 1940's, company growth in the 1950's and early 1960's was mainly in products based on these three traditional raw materials.

COMPANY HISTORY

Standard Chemical was founded in 1910 through the merger of two medium-sized chemical companies. The company's growth since that time followed a pattern of expansion and consolidation reflecting both economic conditions and the composition of its top management group.

In about 1915, a group of young executives moved into Standard Chemical's top managment. During World War I, the company was very profitable and in the decade that followed, it diversified its range of products and added chemicals based on new kinds of raw materials. The young top management was active and aggressive in seeking out new opportunities. In fact, for a brief period of time during the 20's there was a department which could be likened to a New Venture Division. This top management group stayed in control through the Depression and World War II. The 30's was a period of consolidation forced on the company by general economic conditions. In the 40's, growth was confined to the traditional areas as this first generation of top management grew older and more conservative.

In the late 40's, Standard Chemical reseachers invented a new chemical process which they believed to have great potential. Management would not make a major financial commitment to this innovation, preferring to license it to other chemical companies. In the early 50's, when this process had gained greater acceptance, Standard Chemical entered the business, but on a very conservative scale. Competitiors followed more aggressive strategies building larger, lower cost plants. Because of top management's conservatism, Standard

Chemical lost an opportunity to dominate what developed into a major segment of the chemical industry.

The late 40's was a frustrating period for the younger managers in the company. They saw opportunities which were passed by because of top management risk aversion. This period had an important impact in shaping their attitudes and philosophy and was reflected in the more aggressive positions they later took in expanding capacity in growing new products.

In the early 1950's, a second generation of managers were promoted to the executive committee. Like the members of the Executive Committee whom they replaced, they were a "generation" of managers--almost all were of one age group and had advanced through the company together. Several individuals in Standard Chemical observed that the company's pattern of growth--waves of expansion and consolidation--corresponded to the changes in the composition of the Executive Committee. The company expanded progressively when a new generation of managers moved up to the executive committee. As they became older and more conservative, the company moved into a consolidation phase which ended when a new generation of managers was promoted to the committee.

Development of PVT and DAYLIN

During the 50's, two important new products were developed-- PVT, a plastic and DAYLIN, a synthetic fiber. (Both are ficticious product names.) Standard Chemical took a leading position in both of these products. In 1954, the company built the first US plant for DAYLIN which appeared to have promising growth potential. However, the market did not develop as fast as expected and the plant did not reach capacity until six years later. Similarly, it was difficult to estimate the market potential for PVT and the rate at which demand would increase. Thus, even though Standard Chemical was able to maintain a leading position in both products through the early 60's, their future potential was uncertain.

Change in Top Management

During the 40's and 50's, Standard Chemical's chief executives were individuals who "led by consensus." They did not dominate the Executive Committee but rather sought and followed the views of the majority. This management style brought a carefully weighed corporate strategy--balanced, moderate growth, and diversification into closely related areas.

In 1962, a third generation of management took control. Ken Anderson, General Manager of the International Division, was selected to be President. This marked a major break with the traditional pattern of top management succession. Prior to that, Standard Chemical's president had always been chosen from the ranks of the Executive Committee, a level in the organization directly above division general managers. In fact, up until the early 60's promotion within the top ranks of the company was based almost entirely on seniority. When a vacancy opened up on the executive committee, it was said that the division general manager with the most seniority would sit by his telephone and wait for the call.

Ken Anderson posed a marked contrast to Standard Chemical's earlier presidents. He was a dynamic and aggressive individual. He was described as "a very strong president who had vision, was articulate and strong willed."

As General Manager of the International Division, he had seen the overseas potential for Standard Chemicals in the 50's and had earned his reputation by presiding over the rapid growth of that division.

ESTABLISHMENT OF NVD

In 1968, Ken Anderson proposed the formation of a New Venture Division and he became its chief proponent. The Executive Committee supported the idea of a New Venture Division because of both Ken Anderson's strong conviction and the logic of the argument he presented. Those members of the Executive Committee who were not in favor of the New Venture Division deferred to the others because "it was not an important enough issue to split the committee."

Rationale for NVD

There were several reasons for forming the New Venture Division. The president and Executive Committee had reviewed Standard Chemical's long range plans and recognized that forecasted cash flow exceeded forecasted investment opportunities in their existing businesses. The New Venture Division was intended to generate investment opportunities to close this "investment gap."

A second reason for establishing the New Venture Division was a desire to diversify. Standard Chemical had historically diversified into related areas in the chemical industry rather than into businesses which were radically new or unrelated. This had been done primarily by acquiring companies with a new technology or product and improving it through research and development and marketing it effectively. However, the growth of the chemical industry appeared to be flattening out and was not expected to be sufficient to meet management's objective of 10% growth per year.

In addition, the chemical industry was becoming more competitive. One individual in the New Venture Division observed:

> "It was a time when the chemical industry thought every business in the country was good except for the chemical business. The oil companies had stuck their foot into the chemical industry and ruined the pricing structure without anyone having made any money out of it. They were playing around in our industry like it was a gas war."

A third reason for establishing the New Venture Division was that Standard Chemical's growth businesses of the 1950's and 1960's were maturing. PVT and DAYLIN which provided most of the growth in the 70's were at that time not perceived as major growth businesses. The former looked like a long term gamble with an uncertian payoff while the latter appeared already to be maturing.

A fourth reason for forming the New Venture Division was a feeling within top management that the company was not effective in bringing new businesses or new products out of corporate research even though approximately 20% of Standard Chemical's research budget was spent in the corporate research facility. A specific problem was that potential products developed in corporate research did not get commercial sponsorship unless they were related to the existing products or markets of an operating department. Thus, it was believed that some promising new products were falling between divisional lines. Standard Chemical's divisional research and development had traditionally been evolutionary, emphasizing product improvements and process improvements. The company's strength as one executive stated had been "not in invention, but rather in improving upon existing products." It was felt that the New Venture Division could be a mechanism for commercializing corporate research developments which were outside of existing product lines.

A fifth reason for establishing the New Venture Division was that other companies were setting up venture groups. Several chemical companies were making "rumblings" about diversifying out of the industry. The venture groups at DuPont and other chemical companies were spending heavily and widely publicized.

Another reason for establishing the New Venture Division was the belief that Standard Chemical was ripe for a takeover attempt. Several times in the middle 50's, Ken Anderson had expressed concern about the possibility of a "raid." The company's balance sheet was very strong, it had a large cash flow and the existing base did not provide sufficient opportunities to consume this cash flow. One purpose for having the New Venture Division was to rectify this situation.

Three other factors also played a role in the decision to establish the New Venture Division. These were rising corporate profits, the entrepreneurial orientation of the company's president--Ken Anderson, and a desire to improve Standard Chemical's public image.

Staffing of NVD

Dr. Arthur Paulson was chosen by Ken Anderson to be the first General Manager of the New Venture Division. Dr. Paulson had been with Standard Chemical for 18 years and had served in several positions in research, sales, and commercial development. Prior to being appointed General Manager of the New Venture Division, he had been chosen by Ken Anderson to head an "exploration and evaluation" team which investigated acquisitions and joint ventures carried out at the corporate level. He had developed a reputation for competence in that type of work.

Most of the individuals on his staff had also been with the company for many years. He tried to get a cross section of experience, functions, and education. He also attempted to get representation from different divisions of the company. The president wanted all of the existing divisions to have a say in which direction the company was moving and felt this would broaden support for the New Venture Division. Another reason for the desire to have a broad selection of individuals was Dr. Paulson's view that there were quite a few qualified and intelligent people available in each of the divisions. He used the New Venture Division to pull "bright stars" from the operating divisions. He felt that resistance to this was minimized because the operating divisions realized that these individuals would probably eventually be coming back, possibly as venture managers.

Several of the individuals in the NVD were drawn from the Research division. Prior to the establishment of the NVD, there had been a Development group in Standard Chemical's Research division. Most of the staff of this group, and its three major projects were transferrred to the NVD.

In addition to individuals from the operating division and Research division, there were a number of people who had primarily staff experience. During the 1960's, there had been a staff group responsible for acquisition. This was incorporated into the New Venture Division. Most of the planning and futures oriented staff people ended up in the New Venture Division as well. A member of the New Venture Division explained:

"Like most companies, we have always had a department or committee looking at where the company would go beyond its normal business. This function continues to be performed, but the group which does it, or the name it is given seems to change every four or five years. Ten years ago, the corporate planning department was doing it. After that, we had a committee which was primarily acquisition oriented and then we had the New Venture Division. Many of the people in the New Venture Division had been in the corporate planning department earlier. When you read the press releases, it might seem like the New Venture Division was a brand new bright idea. But when you look at the staffing, you realize that it included many of the same futures oriented staff people."

NVD OBJECTIVES AND APPROACH

The New Venture Division was guided by the objective of making a major impact on Standard Chemical in both sales and profit. In fact, the New Venture Division was expected to play a primary role in filling the company's "growth gap" projected for the 1970's. This was described in the New Venture Division's 1971 three-year plan:

"The New Venture Division's three year plan must relate to the accepted growth need of Standard Chemical. If a 10% Inherent Growth Rate objective is adopted for 1980, our program for 1971-1973 should aim to fill a major part of the "growth gap" of approximately $1,000 million sales in new high profit businesses for 1980. . .

Our estimate of the potential 1980 sales for new businesses already started (leaves a) "residual gap" of $550 million sales to be generated from new businesses not yet defined for action. . .The New Venture Division's program should place major emphasis on the following. . . making small but hopefully significant beginning steps in New Venture Division type venture businesses so that when capital is available, the growth opportunities of the late seventies are ready."

The New Venture Division's plans were dominated by financial language and potential ventures were evaluated in terms of their expected contribution of closing the "gap" in projected sales and earnings. An individual in the New Venture Division explained how they thought of ventures:

"We used to talk of a "planning gap" between the goals of the corporation and the projections of the existing businesses. When we looked at potential business opportunities, we thought of them in relation to this gap."

The size of a venture and its potential impact on earnings was often seen as more important than its ultimate cost or its likelihood of success. In other words "expected profit" was a more important consideration than "probability of success." A participant in the New Venture Division explained this:

> "None of our ventures were as big as I would like to have had them. There were pressures to produce large ventures that could contribute significantly to corporate earnings and sales. These large ventures may not have had the best chance to succeed, but they had the best chance to contribute to earnings and sales. Small projects dissipate your efforts and consume excess effort in relation to their profit contribution. With small ventures you may be a success in one way--you have a profitable venture--but you are a failure when it comes to finding ventures that significantly turn or modify the company."

Thus it was decided that if the New Venture Division was going to make a contribution to closing the gap, it had to look at businesses with at least $20 million potential within five years--"hopefully," three to five times that and the sooner the better."

Harry Warren, the Development Manager for the New Venture Division had responsibility for the evaluation and screening of potential start-up ventures. He described the criteria which guided his search:

> "One of the most important things was the total size--what would be the potential contribution to earnings per share of the venture as a mature business? Secondly, what is the projected return on investment? Third, what's the cash flow projection look like? How deep is the trough before we come out of it? Fourth, what does Standard Chemical bring to the business? Fifth, how protected or proprietary is it?"

An important criteria was that the cumulative negative cash flow for a single venture should not exceed five million dollars, including a modest investment and operating losses. At a future point, if the venture was doing well, it would be possible to make a larger capital investment. They also sought a high technological input in their ventures, either in chemistry, physics, or engineering. They estimated that it would take about five years for cumulative cash flow to break even (net out to zero). Ed Lunt, a former General Manager of the New Venture Division stated:

> "Everybody hopes they can find a way to commercialize a new technology in three to five years. I haven't found it yet. That's what we were hoping we could do. We thought we could shortcut the whole thing by being smarter and picking the right areas to go

into. But, in the New Venture Division we were trying to pull together long term research and long term environmental scanning, and that's a long term job."

After accumulating some experience, the forecasted breakeven period was lengthened to eight years. Dr. Paulson explained:

"Where ventures fall down in misreading the market is in timing. The problem is not whether the market will fail to ever develop or accept a product, but that the venture needs the financial resources to wait for that to happen. It is important to know how much it will really take to get the venture off the ground. Even then it will occasionally miss on a technical problem."

Idea Generating

The New Venture Division attempted to identify in broad terms market opportunities which Standard Chemicals could pursue. Most ventures grew out of suggestions originating in the New Venture Division. The approach was to have individuals in the New Venture Division identify growth areas and make recommendations for how Standard Chemicals could participate in these markets. The individuals conducting the venture generating activity attempted to look at the total business environment and break it down into segments such as housing, food, and recreation. Then they tried to define what was going on in each field and determine what approaches were appropriate for entry.

The selection of areas of interest was based on both an analysis of company strengths and weaknesses as well as the evaluation of opportunities that came to the NVD's attention. There were situations where the emergence of an opportunity (i.e., to buy a company or acquire technology) exposed the New Venture Division to an industry which had not been studied. They would then begin to explore this new area. However, the basic thrust of their venture generating activity was to match strengths to future growth opportunities. In most cases, venture ideas were derived from that systematic scanning, surveillance, and analysis activity.

In time, the New Venture Division identified several broad areas which their ventures would aim at. These included: 1) specialty fabric products, 2) printing and photochemical products, 3) electro-optical information systems, 4) bio-medical and health products, and 5) modular housing. Other areas which had been considered included industrial and vehicle safety, pharmaceutical, oil and furniture.

Entry Strategy

The New Venture Division attempted to take a several-pronged approach towards entering the four selected areas, including acquisition, start-ups, and minority equity investments. All were to be pursued along the five major diversification thrusts. The New Venture Division's 1971 three-year plan explained the logic behind this "shotgun" approach:

> "The odds against any venture being very successful are relatively high.....Consequently, a large number of ventures must be "seeded" to enable a few with the required profitability to emerge."

A major reason for the multi-pronged entrance strategy rather than only start-up ventures was to achieve a faster "cycle time," so that the department's work could be justified on a discounted cash flow basis. It was thought that the long time required to develop a new business to the point that it would impact on Standard Chemical could be shortened by merging several compatible ventures. However, it was found that once the ventures were under way they were rarely as compatible as planned. Ed Lunt explained:

> "A real dilemma for us was that something had to be big, $80-100 million, to have an impact on Standard Chemicals. But most of the promising businesses we saw were small. Our solution was to try to coalesce several small ventures. The problem was that once you got into these businesses, you realized that the opportunities to bring them together were limited. It turns out that you are putting together a mini-conglomerate. We discovered that what we thought was 'an industry' was in reality a lot of fragmented markets with very few threads tying them together. When we headed into this, we thought we could pull together several ventures within an industry, but we found out that we just couldn't do it."

Start-up ventures and minority equity investments were the main activities of the New Venture Division. None of the major acquisitions that it recommended were approved by the Executive Committee. Harry Warren, who headed up the group working on start-ups, felt that the pressure on the New Venture Division to make a significant contribution to profits in a relatively short period of time put his group at somewhat of a disadvantage relative to those working on the minority equity and acquisition routes.

In the first two years, six minority equity investments were made. The rationale for the minority equity program was that it would serve as a "widow" on emerging technologies. It was anticipated that at a future date, Standard Chemicals might acquire the remaining equity of some of the companies it was investing in.

There were two major shortcomings that became evident in the minority equity program. The intended "window" did not function effectively. When Standard Chemicals acquired a minority position in a company, only a few people became involved in it--usually a financial man and a technical man--and they "did not really learn the business."

The second shortcoming was that Standard Chemicals Executive Committee was uncomfortable with little control over their investments. Ultimately, most of the minority equity positions were divested.

Venture Spin-Off

The New Venture Division's role was one of both developing opportunities and commercializing them. Once commercialized or semicommercialized, it was planned that ventures and their management would be spun off to operating divisions or set up as new divisions of the company.

EVOLUTION OF THE NVD

The evolution of Standard Chemical's New Venture Division will be described in four phases:

1. 1968 to 1970
2. 1970 to 1972
3. 1972 to 1974
4. 1974 to 1976

1968 to 1970

During the 1968 to 1970 period, the New Venture Division was very active in searching for venture ideas in areas outside of the chemical industry.

Initially the New Venture Division had been given little initial direction by the Executive Committee. It was intended that the New Venture Division would serve a "scouting" function--identifying potential opportunities and submitting these to the Executive Committee for consideration. The mandate from the Executive Committee was: "Bring us options!"

Numerous proposals for acquisitions and minority equity investments were presented to the Executive Committee. The New Venture Division worked on a new proposal "every two or three weeks." The Executive Committee was "patient and listened" but all of the New

Venture Division's acquisition proposals were turned down, although six small minority equity investments were approved.

Dr. Paulson did not have a close working relationship with Ken Anderson. He explained that his "stature in the company at that time did not allow it." The president had little involvement in the preparation of proposals for the Executive Committee or the development of a strategy for the New Venture Division. He simply approved or disapproved proposals which were submitted. The expectations for the New Venture Division and its strategy were thus unclear. One staff member observed:

> "Each division in the company had its own strategy but I never saw a strategy for the corporation as a whole which encompassed us. We developed a New Venture Division strategy for which there was tacit approval, but there was always vacillation."

Dr. Paulson attempted to define "the ground rules" for the New Venture Division, but his only way of doing this was to bring proposals before the Executive Committee and to learn from their reactions. He was "caught in the middle" because he had to present proposals to the Executive Committee to get the New Venture Division's guidelines defined but the continual rejection of proposals weakened the New Venture Division's position.

At one point, Dr. Paulson attempted to resolve this dilemma by asking the Executive Committee for $2,000,000 which the New Venture Division could invest in projects without having to obtain Executive Committee approval for each specific project. He argued that his staff was spending a large portion of their time preparing proposals which were usually turned down.

Dr. Paulson's proposal was strongly opposed by some of the more conservative members of the Executive Committee. It damaged his credibility and what was viewed by some as an "irresponsible request for funds with no documentation" provided a tool for those on the Executive Committee opposed to the New Venture Division approach.

Growth in Size

In the three years 1968-1970, the New Venture Division staff doubled in size. The were organized, as in figure 4-1, into three groups: a Development Group, an Acquisition Group, and a Minority Equity Group. Individual ventures reported to the head of one of these three groups.

As one of the eight division General Managers in Standard Chemicals, the General Manager of the New Venture Division reported

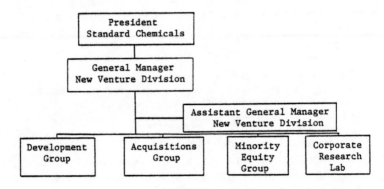

Figure 4-1

to the company President. The organization structure of Standard Chemicals was rather unusual. Although the division managers reported to the President, there were four Vice Presidents on an Executive Committee. Each division had one of these Vice Presidents as an advisor, and they played a role somewhat like that of a Group Vice President, however they had less direct control over operations than a Group Vice President.

Relations with Other Departments

The creation of the New Venture Division was not welcomed by the operating divisions. It was felt by those opposed to the NVD that the New Venture Division was unnecessary and that future growth opportunities could develop through both expanison into international markets which were beginning to open up and through forward integration (increasing value added) and product line extensions.

A third objection to the New Venture Division was what one Executive Committee member referred to as the "price of success." The New Venture Division was a potential competitor for capital--"another mount to feed." If it was successful in launching ventures, funding their expansion could draw substantial capital away from the existing operation divisions.

The formation of the New Venture Division was characterized by high exposure and high expectations. The New Venture Division was a "hot area." It was in the limelight--featured in the company magazine and annual report. This served to generate the unrealistic expectations.

It also created the kind of jealousy and resentment in the company which normally accompanies a creation of a new area which is given undue attention. However, this was magnified by what one inivndual called Ken Anderson's "kiss of death" to the New Venture Division. In public statements, the president often referred to it "the brightest young people in the company." Several individuals commented that this oft-repeated phrase was the source of much of the resentment that developed toward the New Venture Division.

Although there were no obvious direct attempts to undermine the New Venture Division, there was little grass roots support for it in the company. The "pot shots" taken at the New Venture Division were in the form of withheld support--a reluctance to cooperate or lend it assistance. This was felt by New Venture Division members almost from its first day. In addition there was criticism of the New Venture Division "behind closed doors."

It was noted that when the NVD was working on a project that would be spun off, there was better cooperation from the division that would be the recipient of the venture. However, this was the exception, as most of the ventures did not fit into an operating division and were either to be retained in the NVD or set up as separate divisions.

The New Venture Division was relatively self-sufficient and thus there was little dependence on or interaction with the operating divisions. This was especially so in the period 1968-1972 when the NVD was pursuing ventures relatively far afield. The resources of the operating divisions usually were not relevant to these unrelated businesses.

Relations with the corporate staff departments varied. Relations with the corporate Accounting and Legal departments were better than those with the Corporate Treasurer and the Engineering department. The Legal department assigned a lawyer to serve as legal advisor to the NVD. He spent nearly all of his time assisting the New Venture Division.

The Corporate Treasurer, however, was a leading critic of the New Venture Division. He felt that supporting the New Venture Division's activities was an unwise investment of corporate funds when alternative more secure opportunities existed.

Ken Anderson's Support

After the New Venture Division was established, Ken Anderson provided strong support for it in several ways. He helped staff it by recruiting some individuals, "opening the doors" for Dr. Paulson, and helping him "get by the resistance of the division general managers" to recruit others.

He also assured funding by gaining the approval of the Executive Committee for the amount he felt was appropriate. In addition, he provided flexibility in the budget by allowing the inclusion of funds which were not allocated to a specific purpose.

One member of the Executive Committe observed that during the first few years of the New Venture Division's existence, Ken Anderson could be counted on to support its proposals to the committee "as long as they were within reasonable bounds." This was important as the Executive Committee was fairly evenly divided with respect to the New Venture Division. Of seven members, three plus the president could usually be counted on in favor of New Venture Division proposals, two were almost always firmly opposed and a third was usually among the opposition. Thus even when not actively persuading others, Ken Anderson was often in the position of the swing vote with respect to the New Venture Division.

Relations with Research Division

The relations between the NVD and the Standard Chemicals Research division were especially important as this division was the source of several venture ideas and provided input for others.

In 1968 Standard Chemical's Research division operated a corporate research facility which housed divisional research departments, three corporate support groups (Analytical, Chemical Engineering, and Applications Research), and an Advanced Research department which conducted "basic" research in chemistry. All of these research groups, including those of the divisions, reported to the Director of the Research division who in turn reported to the Executive Committee.

Within the NVD, there was no research department. The three development projects brought to the NVD from the Research division required laboratory work and this was accomplished by using Research division personnel and charging their costs to the NVD. Relations between the NVD and the Research division were facilitated by the fact that the manager of the Development group within the NVD had previously worked in the Applications Research group in the Research division. He drew on his old department (Applications Research) both because he felt their skills fit the needs of the ventures and because of his good relationships with the researchers there.

Modular Housing

The major output of the 1968-1970 period was a combined start-up venture/minority equity investment/acquisition in modular housing which was launched in 1969. An individual in the New Venture Division explained how the idea developed:

> "At the time the whole housing industry was getting a lot of attention. Everybody was looking at it including, GE, Westinghouse, and Fruehauf. In the New Venture Division we were looking for new areas to go into. I began looking at building materials, then looked at mobile homes and finally ended up in modular housing.'

> "Modular housing looked very attractive not only to us but to these other companies because we were all working with the same assumption--that the high labor costs of stick building were such that you could produce houses more economically in a plant."

In May 1969, the New Venture Division made a minority investment in a small company in the industry (Checco Construction Company) as a "window" on a modular housing. About ten months later, the New Venture Division obtained Standard Chemical board's approval to enter the modular housing industry. This approval was for acquiring the remaining equity in the real estate development company (approximately $1.0 million) and building a plant with a capacity of 1,000 homes per year on a one shift, five day per week basis (approximately $1.5 million). These two steps were considered the first phase of what could eventually develop into a $200-300 million business. At that point (April 1970) the venture was spun-off from the New Venture Division and was set up as a separate unit reporting directly to the Executive Committee. It was felt that it was of sufficient size to warrant close attention by top management.

Standard Chemical's experience with this venture became a critical factor influencing the evolution of the NVD. The failure of this venture (described later in this chapter) led to management disillusionment with the concept of venturing as well as a questioning of whether Standard Chemical should attempt to diversify into areas outside of the chemical industry.

Summary

The period of 1968 to 1970 was characterized by the increasing activity, prominence, and visibility of the New Venture Division. Ken Anderson was firmly in control as President of Standard Chemical and he assured that the New Venture Division activity continued to be high-lighted. Nevertheless, toward the end of this period pressures on the New Venture Division began to grow. It had produced only one large venture with no positive impact on Standard Chemical and changes were taking place which were creating a misfit between the New Venture Division's mission and the company's business situation.

1970 to 1972

Corporate Situation

In 1969 demand "began to take off" for two relatively small products in which Standard Chemical had a leading position: DAYLIN and PVT. The growth in demand of these two products was "amazing" and Standard Chemicals responded by "committing large chunks of capital" to expand capacity. In a period of two years, 1969 and 1970, the logic of Standard Chemical's position shifted dramatically. Instead of being a mature business with limited opportunities, the company found itself with two growth businesses and the question became "how will we keep up with them?"

The Executive Committee recognized the new situation the company was in. The members of the Executive Committee in the early 1970's were the frustrated young managers of the late 1940's, and were well aware of the opportunity costs of excess conservatism. In both DAYLIN and PVT they were in a position to dominate the business. By expanding aggressively, they could capitalize on their leading position. One member of the Executive Committee explained:

> "The psychology on the Executive Committee changed completely. Instead of searching for new oppor- tunities, we had to start selecting which games we wanted to play in."

The capital demands of these two growing businesses and tightening credit markets affected the company's financial position over the four year period from 1970 to 1974. The excess cash flow which prompted the establishment of the New Venture Division was a thing of the past and by 1973 the company was in a capital rationing position. Capital expenditures in 1973 were nearly triple those in 1971. In 1974 they were 50% higher or more than four times the 1971 level. Long-term debt increased by approximately 40% from 1972 to 1973 and in 1974 it nearly doubled the 1973 level. Standard Chemical's debt-equity ratio increased from 25% in 1972 to over 50% in 1974 (See Appendix 4-1).

In 1970 and 1971, there were major changes in Standard Chemical's top management. Willis Keenan replaced Ken Anderson as

President in mid-1970. Keenan's management style differed from his prodecessor. Whereas Ken Anderson was described as entrepreneurial, Will Keenan was a more conservative, "judicial" leader. He "listened to the Executive Committee" and was influenced to a greater extent by the opinions of other members--thus, he tended to follow the consensus arrived at by the committee rather than imposing his own views on it.

At this time, there was "a flock of resignations" from the Executive Committee. It was reduced in size from ten members to five as a "generation of top managers" retired.

The "new" president and Executive Committee believed that Standard Chemical should not pursue a strategy of "unrelated" diversification but rather return to its traditional strategy of diversifying into related areas within the chemical industry.

Experience with Modular Housing

By mid-1970, top management was becoming disillusioned with the Modular Housing venture. The Checco Construction Company which had been acquired in March 1970 was not meeting expectations. The company's management, characterized as "flashy idea men and promoters" did not fit in Standard Chemical. An on-going project inherited with Checco Construction Company encountered "some surprises of a legal nature" (relating to design deficiencies) which highlighted to Standard Chemical's managment their continuing liability even after completion of a project. There was a growing recognition that this type of business did not fit Standard Chemical's values. The members of the Executive Committee had pride in their product and were used to "walking into our customers with our chins high." One member explained their reaction to modular housing:

> "Most of us lived in houses which cost well into six figures. The Executive Committee members would look at our modular housing development and say, 'This is junk.' It was not the type of industry for us. Everybody had their hand out looking for a bribe and that is not how we do business."

Thus, even before the Modular Housing plant was in operation, the experiences with the Checco Construction Company and the projects inherited with it raised doubts about this venture and the company's diversification outside of the chemical industry. As one member of the Executive Committee explained:

> "After venturing into modular housing, the chemical industry looked a lot more attractive."

By the beginning of 1972, Modular Housing was running into financial difficulties. There had been a gradual erosion of the original assumptions, growing problems and accumulating losses. In June 1972, the Executive Committee decided to discontinue the venture. It could not be sold as a going business and was liquidated.

Standard Chemical's early dissatisfaction with the Modular Housing venture was a critical event which influenced the Executive Committee's thinking with respect to corporate strategy. A member of the Executive Committee explained:

> "The overriding reason for the shift in our thinking was the emergence of PVT and DAYLIN, but the proximate reason was our experience with Modular Housing."

The Executive Committee saw the Modular Housing venture as a failure. They felt that they had overpaid for the Checco Construction Company acquisition and in less than one year of full operation the venture had lost almost $5 million. In addition, it had become clear that the typical practices of the real estate and construction businesses did not fit with the dominant values of Standard Chemical.

Change in Corporate Strategy

In January, 1971, Will Keenan indicated a desire to modify Standard Chemical's diversification strategy. At the company's annual planning conference at which the divisional general managers and Executive Committee met for several days at a retreat, he issued a challenge to the operating divisions. He asked them how they could fill the company's "planning gap."

One year later at the next planning conference (January, 1972), the general managers of the operating divisions responded by presenting plans as to how they would generate the sales and profits to fill this gap.

This one year period thus marked a fundamental shift in Standard Chemical's corporate strategy from one of unrelated diversification carried out by a New Venture Division to one of related diversification carried out by the operating divisions.

Modification of NVD Mission

The changes in top management and the shift in corporate strategy impacted on the New Venture Division. But, their effect was gradual--they brought evolutionary changes in the New Venture Division. Its stated mission was not immediately altered by top management as the president and Executive Committee had more pressing matters to deal with. A member of the Executive Committee explained:

> "In 1971, the Executive Committee had perhaps thirty problems it was dealing with. Of those, the New Venture Division was down in the twenties. It was not really costing a lot of money and we had more important things to concentrate on."

Indirectly, however, the changing corporate situation was felt by the New Venture Division. Pressures for the initiation of ventures which would make a "impact on the company" lessened as it became clear that the operating divisions were going to have primary responsibility for filling the "planning gap"--with the New Venture Division playing a supplementary role. This "took some of the heat off" the New Venture Division. Will Keenan had never believed that it should "or could" play the primary role in filling the "gap" and the New Venture Division began to take on a different identity more in tune with his view of what it should be.

The approach to generating venture ideas was also modified. "Related" ventures which built on existing company skills and capabilities were sought. Rather than scanning the environment for the most glamorous and fastest growing industries, the NVD focused its search inward for product ideas already existing within the company. This change in the type of venture sought is illustrated later in this chapter by a comparison of the Modular Housing venture and the Lithomer venture, which was launched in 1972.

Closer Ties with Advanced Research

In 1972, the Advanced Research group was transferred from the Research division to the NVD where it reported to the General Manager. During the 1968-1971 period, this group of about 25 researchers had begun to feel "out in left field." They saw the corporation pursuing ventures in unrelated areas and "were wondering where their skills in chemistry fit into this picture."

The purpose of this organizational change was to provide direction for Advanced Research and to "coordinate the total long term new direction efforts of the company." In addition, the General Manager of the NVD met occasionally with the Research division to talk about objectives and to follow the progress of various programs.

There had previously been some interaction between the NVD and Advanced Research but it had been limited because the skills of the group did not fit the needs of the ventures. This change in organization brought greater involvement of Advanced Research in NVD activies and vice versa. The NVD was given more responsibility for planning and market assessment of the corporate research effort. The change in organization also brought the Advanced Research group a little closer to the market although there was no major change in their basic research orientation.

The increased coordination between the NVD and Advanced Research reflected the shift of the NVD toward more related ventures for which the knowledge of corporate researchers was more relevant.

Although this organizational change expanded the scope of the NVD's mission, it also marked the beginning of a gradual evolution of the NVD toward a staff function--planning and analysis which would eventually replace the commercialization of ventures as its function.

Lithomer Venture

In 1972, the New Venture Division's second major start-up venture introduced its product commercially.[1] The venture, called Lithomer, aimed at developing of lithographic plate-making systems for newspaper printing presses.

This venture was based on a product licensed from a Japanese firm in 1969. Standard Chemical's Research Department and then the NVD had been studying the market for this product and related technologies for several years. Over the next two years, Standard Chemical improved on this technology and the Lithomer system was introduced commercially in June 1972. This venture had been relatively successful and in 1976 it appeared that it had a sales potential of over $100 million. It was operating at about break-even, but sales were increasing rapidly.

The Lithomer venture posed a marked contrast to the earlier Modular Housing venture. The difference was indicative of the shift in the NVD's mission. The Modular Housing venture had been an attempt to enter a glamorous industry unrelated to Standard Chemical's existing products, markets or technology. By 1972, when the Lithomer system was introduced, the mission of the NVD had evolved and ventures "closer to home" (and perhaps less glamorous) were sought. An individual who was in the New Venture Division at the time explained how Lithomer fit with the changing direction of the New Venture Division:

"In 1971 and 1972, the direction of the department began to change. We decided that we were going too far out and we were overlooking plenty of opportunities closer to home. That's when we focused on

Lithomer. We said 'that's the one which will fit with the gut feel of Standard Chemical. It's chemistry and we can add to it.'"

Conflict with Corporate Engineering

In 1972, Lithomer became the center of a major conflict which developed between the corporate engineering department and the New Venture Division. Early in the venture, problems arose over mounting the Lithomer plates on the printing presses. The venture drew on corporate engineering for assistance. Over the next year, conflicts developed between the two departments as the New Venture Division gradually came to the conclusion that the required mechanical engineering skills were not available in the corporate engineering department. Corporate Engineering had experience and knowledge in process engineering for the chemical industry but this did not fit with the needs of the venture. Over the next few years, the venture gradually hired mechanical engineers and built up an internal engineering function. This violated corporate policy, but was gradually accepted as the need for a separate engineering group in the venture became clear.

Summary

During the period 1970-1972, a clear misfit developed between the mission of the NVD and Standard Chemical's corporate situation. Two high growth products emerged, the outlook for the chemical industry brightened, top management became more conservative, and the projected funds surplus disappeared as capital expenditures expanded dramatically. The NVD slowly began to respond to this new situation evolving toward a mission of more related diversification and taking on an increased staff function of planning and market assessment for advanced research.

1972 to 1974

The period from 1972 to 1974 was one of transition for the New Venture Division. A misfit had developed between the New Venture Division's earlier role and Standard Chemical's corporate strategy. The New Venture Division gradually declined in size and importance during this period and its venture generating activities were wound down.

Turnover of General Managers

In mid-1972, Dr. Arthur Paulson was appointed General Manager of one of Standard Chemical's operating divisions and Robert

Zucker replaced him as General Manager of the New Venture Division. This began a two year period of high turnover in the top position of the NVD. (Robert Zucker held the position for ten months before being appointed General Manager of Standard Chemical's International Division. In June, 1973, Ed Lunt became General Manager of the New Venture Division, but he also held the position for less than a year. In March, 1974, he was replaced by Bill Hennesey). An individual who had been in the New Venture Division for most of this period commented:

> "This turnover reflected the lack of a strong commitment on the part of the Executive Committee. They began to view the New Venture Division as a department which needed a little attention. The people assigned to head up the New Venture Division were all 'comers.' They put them in charge of the New Venture Division until a position opened up for them."

Related Diversification

By the end of 1972, the corporate strategy of pursuing related diversification--growing within the chemical industry--was appearing better and better. PVT and DAYLIN were continuing their tremendous growth and the major investments in new facilities which were made under Ken Anderson in the late 160's were beginning to pay off. The years 1972 to 1974 were banner years and this made the chemical industry look a lot more attractive.

New Mission

In early 1973 the Executive Committee gave the New Venture Division a new charter. It was told to pursue only related ventures and to begin divesting ventures outside of the chemical industry. During the next two years, the New Venture Division carried out a combined function of attempting to find markets for products that had been developed in the corporate research facility, divesting unrelated ventures, serving as a training ground for divisional general managers (where they could be put in a holding pattern until a position opened up) and managing Standard Chemical's participation in a joint venture in pharmaceuticals.

Robert Zucker had a particular interest in this joint venture which had developed in 1972 shortly after he took over the New Venture Division. During his tenure of ten months, the department was without a clear mission and this joint venture became its main activity.

When Ed Lunt took over in June 1973, he directed the New Venture Division's efforts toward opportunities within the chemical industry and began to carry out the divestment charter he had been given by the Executive Committee. He explained:

> "What I was doing during this period was sweeping up. We began to call those high technology companies that we had bought minority positions in 'cottage industries.' We got out of them and started aiming at our own type of business."

1974 to 1976

In March, 1974, Ed Lunt was replaced by Bill Hennesey, who was given the assignment "to re-evaluate the New Venture Division." He explained:

> "I was given the charter to look at the New Venture Division very critically--should it be changed, shut down or what? When I took over there was no expectation that I would initiate new ventures. I was to be evaluated on the basis of what kind of plan I came up with to change the direction of the division. The corporation was dissatisfied with the New Venture Division. They looked back on a long history of failures and said 'What do we need this for?' The reason for setting up the New Venture Division--mainly that there were limited opportunities in the chemical industry--had completely vanished. The President who set it up had retired. I spent my time trying to find buyers for some ventures, trying to figure out whether to step up or shut down others and trying to find a home in our operating divisions for a third group."

Redefinition

In January, 1975, the role of the New Venture Division was changed to a staff function. Bill Henessey was made General Manager of an operating division and the individual replacing him was given the title, "Director--New Venture Department" rather than "General- Manager--New Venture Division."

The individual who had headed up the Development group within the NVD returned to the Research division and the Advanced Research department was also transferred to the Research division. This was described as "all part of a transition to turn our attention back to the Chemical industry."

The New Venture Department's responsibilities in 1975 included business planning, review of investment projects over a given size, and identification and analysis of potential acquisitions. The New Venture Department no longer had responsibility for launching new ventures. It had been replaced in this function by a formal corporate-wide program in which long term development projects carried out by the divisions were corporately financed.

Although the New Venture Department was no longer responsible for Advanced Research, it did continue to assist in market assessment and market development but to a much lesser extent than in prior years.

Gradual Evolution

In reflecting back on the evolution of the New Venture Division, one long time department member observed:

> "Initially, the New Venture Division had a charter to start ventures and make acquisitions in new areas. It soon began to perform a service function for the divisions in the acquisition area. The question of how far afield we were going to go with our ventures was starting to be resolved. When you stay closer to home, the operating departments have more to say, and there is increased pressure for the ventures to be transferred out of the New Venture Division. It limits how much the New Venture Division can do on its own. Also, the first generation of ventures gradually were spun off and the number of people who were looking to generate new ones decreased. It became a staff function in 1975, but in retrospect I think it was moving in that direction before then."

The role of the New Venture Department in 1976 reflected the changes taking place in the chemical industry. The member of the Executive Committee to whom the department reported explained that structural changes in the chemical industry warranted an entirely different strategy than was followed a decade earlier:

> "The American chemical industry is now much more just a part of the world industry. A decade ago, five of the ten top chemical companies were American. Today only three are. The increased world-wide competition means that you have to concentrate on certain products and serve the international market with them. Instead of having 15 products in the U.S., you are in a better position with seven products worldwide. Companies that are our size now have to stay with what they are good at and either be a big force in the world with those products or get out."

Given this assessment of the industry, strategic evaluation and planning are more important corporate functions than the generation of new businesses. In 1976, the primary role of the New Venture

Department--business planning--fit with the Executive Committee's assessment of the industry situation and its strategy for Standard Chemical.

NOTES

[1]Several other start-up ventures had been carried into a development stage but had not been introduced commercially. Two of the three development projects inherited from the corporate Research Division were discontinued. Lithomer was the third.

CHAPTER 5

DUPONT COMPANY DEVELOPMENT DEPARTMENT

Evolution from 1960 to 1976

In 1976, DuPont Company was the largest U.S. chemical producer with revenues of over 7 billion dollars annually. In 1976, the Company's broadly diversified product line included both industrial and consumer products and included synthetic fibers, paint, agricultural chemicals and medical instruments.

During the period 1953-1974, DuPont's sales increased more than four-fold and net income doubled. Most of this growth occurred in markets in which the company had attained a leading position through the introduction of innovative new products--either internally developed or purchased through the acquisition of small companies.

Company History

To understand the evolution of DuPont's new venture activities it is necessary to take an historical perspective of the company's development.

DuPont had been a leading company in the United States chemical industry since the early 1900's. During World War I, the company more than tripled in size and was very profitable. In the 1920's, the expansion of the previous decade was absorbed and consolidated and DuPont began to diversify into new areas within the chemical industry.

The company was family owned and managed at this time and top management was young. This was significant as it allowed them to develop a long range plan for growth and diversification with the expectation that they would be in control to see this plan carried out over the following two decades.

In the diversification program of the 1920's, several small companies with promising new technologies were acquired. The technologies acquired during this period were seen as the levers for opening up broad potential markets which could be developed and expanded in the future. Most of these companies remained small for more than a decade before blossoming into the growth businesses of the late 40's and 50's. On the average at DuPont, it had taken 23 years for a new product to reach sales of $50 million.

During the 1940's, the technologies acquired in the 20's were integrated into the company. "Pioneering" research was centralized and this brought about much cross-fertilization of process and chemical knowledge.

The 50's was a very profitable "growth decade" for the company as it realized the payoff from the innovative products acquired and developed in the 20's. Increasing demand for these products, the development of closely related product line extensions, and the discovery of new applications for products and technologies already existing in the company all contributed to the growth of the 50's.

Corporate Culture

Within DuPont there was a strong corporate culture and sense of identity which strongly influenced the evolution of both the company and its new venture activities. DuPont's corporate culture was characterized by the following:

Research and Development Orientation

Historically, the company had achieved market penetration and dominance by having technologically innovative products. DuPont's approach to diversification in the past had been to acquire technology and/or to internally develop innovative products. During the late sixties, approximately $250 million annually was spent on research and development. The company had a very high percentage of individuals with advanced degrees in the sciences, its salaries for researchers was above average and it was known to have one of the best research capabilities in American industry. Its compensation system supported this R & D orientation by having a system of bonuses which rewarded innovation--particularly that achieved by a "product champion" who successfully overcame the skepticism and resistance of others.

"People" Orientation

The company had a strong concern for its employees. There was an unusually large number of employees who had spent their whole career with the company--many serving thirty or more years. For the most part, its plants were not organized by national unions, its on-the-job accident record was the safest in the industry, and it was the first chemical company to have a major concern about safety. It is important to note that this concern stemmed from an interest in employees' welfare rather than just profit considerations.

Corporate Responsibility

A third core value at DuPont was the company's strong sense of social responsibility and high standards of conduct. These were reflected in the statements of its top management as well as a system of high product standards it set for itself. One member of the executive committee described this characteristic of the company as a "sense of ethical obligation."

Historical Perspective

Among top management, as well as employees at lower levels of the corporation, there was an unusually strong awareness of the company's history. There was an intangible notion of "what would be proper" for DuPont (i.e., technologically innovative products) and this historical perspective exerted an influence on decision makers. It supported and complemented the other core values. For example, DuPont's R & D orientation was reinforced by the belief that Nylon, a product which played a key role in DuPont's growth, had developed out of a "basic" research discovery in the corporate laboratory.

This corporate culture and system of values were shaped to a large extent by the fact that the company was family owned and managed for much of its history.. It was not until the 1970's that the first chief executive outside of the founding family was selected. The values of the DuPont family, which were ahead of their time, were ingrained in the company.

New Venture Divisions

From 1960 through 1976 (the time of this writing) DuPont had an organizataional unit which could be considered a "new venture division"--a department whose primary task was the initiation of new ventures and the management of their early commercialization.

1960-1970:   Development Department

From 1960 to 1970, this function was carried out by the corporate Development department. Traditionally, the role of this department had been to serve as the "staff arm of the Executive Committee"--as a department to provide it with information and special studies as input for policy making and often to take the necessary actions to carry out its policies as well. In the course of DuPont's history, the Development department had thus assumed diverse and varied roles, often combining several functions. During the 1960's, the Development department's primary task was to launch new ventures.

1970-1976:   New Business Opportunities Division (NBO)

In 1970, a subunit was created within the Development department and this new department performed the functions of a "new venture division" from 1970 to 1976. This unit, called the New Business Opportunities Division (NBO) was given primary responsibility for the Development department's new venture activities. As will be described below, the creation of the NBO was more than simply a reorganization. It constituted a fundamentally different approach to launching new ventures, brought about in response to a changing corporate situation and the experience gained from DuPont's venture activities of the 60's.

The evolution of the "new venture divisions"--both the Development department and the NBO--will be described in two sections below. In the first section, the role of the Development department from 1960 to 1970 will be discussed. In the second section, the new venture activities of the 1970's will be discussed, focusing on the New Business Opportunities division which was created within the Development department to handle this function.

1960-1970:   Development Department

In 1960, DuPont was in a very favorable position. It was the dominant company in several segments of the chemical industry. Both sales and earnings were in an upward trend. There was an atmosphere of confidence with positive expectations for the future.

DuPont's financial position was strong in 1960. It had been conservatively managed financially and the high profits of the 1950's had generated funds for which "a significant number of major new investment opportunities were not immediately forthcoming." However, it was becoming apparent that many of the company's businesses were maturing.   The chairman and executive committee recognized that DuPont was beginninng to "saturate its markets; its growth was declining and it had to diversify."

Increase in R&D Expenditures

One response to this situation was to increase expenditures for research at both the corporate and divisional levels. The activities of the

Central Research department were expanded with the objective of making technological breakthroughs from which new businesses could be developed. The logic of this approach was to use research breakthroughs (as opposed to its management skills, financial strength, or existing technological capabilities) as the primary resource the company was going to build on in entering new businesses. Top management clearly saw DuPont as a technologically based company with research the driving force for growth. Comments such as the following were typically found in the annual reports of the 60's:

1. "Research has been the foundation of DuPont's record of innovation in the chemical industry."

2. "As a technically based company, DuPont relies primarily on its own staff of scientists and engineers for the discovery and development of new lines of business."

Diversification

A more basic response to the surplus of funds and maturing of DuPont's businesses was a conscious shift in corporate strategy. This took two forms. The company launched a major international expansion of existing operations and parallel to that it initiated a program of diversification. With respect to the latter, a member of the Executive Committe explained:

"Much like during the 1930's, we put a greater emphasis on diversification. The Executive Committee decided that in addition to the stream of investment opportunities from the divisions, there might be merit in a corporate diversification effort to lead us into new fields and provide investment opportunities."

There was no strong desire to get out of the chemical industry but rather a commitment to look in new directions and to compare what was found in relation to opportunities in existing businesses.

Diversification looked especially attractive because of the company's success with its earlier diversification program. A second factor was the atmosphere of confidence and optimism in the company at the time.

The domestic diversification program was to be carried out through internal development rather than through acquisition. There were two main reasons for this. First, it was felt that because of DuPont's size there would be anti-trust hazards with acquisitions. In the late 50's, the courts had ruled against the company in a major anti-trust case. No violation of law was found but the courts ruled that there was

a "potential" violation.   This case had a major influence on top
management thinking and made them "a little gun-shy of large
acquisitions."   One member of the Executive Committee explained:

> "When you go through a long case like that, it chews up quite a bit
> of corporate assets and time.   After that you are leary of getting
> tangled up again."

A second reason for avoiding major acquisitions was that the
company's past growth had been primarily through internal development
and the acquisition of small companies with technological innovations.
DuPont's past success with this approach weighed in favor of it.

Initiation of New Venture Program

The internal development program was carried out by both the
operating divisions and the corporate Development department which
took on the function of a new venture division.

The operating divisions were encouraged to launch "new
ventures." Efforts to develop new products were labeled "new ventures"
if they met certain established criteria, the most important of which were
size and uniqueness--that it be a sizable effort to develop and introduce a
product which did not already exist in the marketplace.   General
managers of operating divisions could elect to have their major
development efforts labeled "new ventures."   These would thus get
special accounting treatment with their costs carried below the bottom
line of the division's profit and loss statement.   This advantage to the
division was offset by the increased exposure to the Executive Committee
that the venture received (rather than being buried in the operating
division's total activities).   Increased exposure limited the flexibility of
the divisional general manager in handling the venture.

The purpose of this arrangement was twofold.   It encouraged the
divisional general managers to become venturesome, since the
development and commercialization costs of their new ventures would
not penalize the performance of their existing operations.   Secondly, it
helped the Executive Committee keep track of how much venture activity
was being undertaken and how the ventures were performing.

The assignment of the function of a new venture division to the
Development department was a step consistent with that department's
traditional role as the staff arm of the Executive Committee.   In the four
decades prior to 1960, the Development department had assumed
different functions in accordance with the needs of the Executive
Committee.   One member of the committee observed:

"The Development department's roles have ebbed and flowed with what the committee saw as the corporate's needs which were not readily attainable through the operating divisions. In fact, if you look at the changing roles of the Development department you would get a good feel for how DuPont's corporate strategy has changed in the course of our history."

In the early 20's, the Development department had been given the task of proposing new directions which the company should move in. The department came up with a plan for diversification and carried this out during the next decade. From the end of World War II through 1960, the Development department took on various "trouble shooting" types of functions. These included corporate planning, licensing of technology, acting as government liaison, and special studies for the Executive Committee. The latter included studies of the corporate organization, (for example, considering the desirability of combining departments) and more specific projects including analyzing the company's patent position.

In 1960, an Assistant Director of the Development department was appointed and made responsible for the department's new venture activities. The Development department continued its other activities including corporate planning and internal consulting with these responsibilities assigned to another Assistant Director.

Organization and Charter

The organization of the departments in 1960 is shown in figure 5-1.

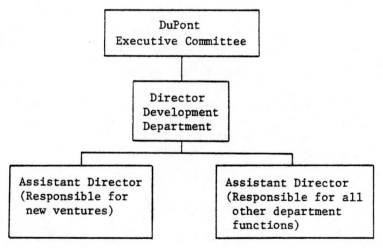

Figure 5-1

The Assistant Director responsible for new ventures was given little initial direction or guidance for how to carry out this function, nor did he have an organization. His first priorities were thus to "put together a staff and determine the bounds of this assignment." He presented the Executive Committee a written paper offering seven ways that the venture activity might be carried out--alternatives such as different types of start-up ventures, minority equity investments and acquisitions of small companies. It was expected that only one or two of these alternatives would be selected. However, the Executive Committee instructed him to pursue all seven approaches. This very positive response was attributed to the Executive Committee's desire to experiment with various approaches and the fact that "things in the business world are fadish" and the approaches offered were somewhat novel.

The corporate-wide venture effort launched in the early sixties was characterized by a lack of specific direction. An individual in an operating department at the firm observed:

> "Top management saw a need for ventures and said 'Go ahead and do it.' Nobody really managed it or directed it. So the whole company began to get into ventures but there was no clear direction or purpose."

Development Department Approach

The diversification program which was implemented consisted of two main thrusts:

1. "Embryonic investment program," consisting of minority equity investments in small, high technology companies.

2. Large scale start-up ventures.

High technology companies to which DuPont could make a contribution in the area of technology were sought. The logic behind this program was that if these companies were successful they would provide one or more of the following:

1. Investment opportunities for DuPont.

2. Businesses to be acquired by DuPont.

3. A synergistic effect through the exchange of technology.

In the start-up venture effort, the Development department sought out "investment opportunities which would use our existing skills and give above average return." There was the hope and expectation that these ventures would have a major impact on corporate earnings. Therefore, the size of the venture and its potential growth were key criteria for selecting ventures. With the limited staff of the Development department, it was not feasible to initiate sufficient number of small ventures to make an impact.

The Development department attempted to generate venture ideas by "looking to the future to determine where there would be abnormal rates of growth and asking how could we get into these areas with our skills and technology." In addition, they kept an "open door" for ideas people wanted to submit from both within the company and outside of it. As part of this, they looked to the operating departments for venture ideas that they failed to back because they were too far out, radical, or unrelated to their existing businesses.

Although the objective was to build on existing company skills-- primaily in house technology and markets they were already serving--the Development department could not pursue ventures which fell within the province of an operating department. Since the company was already well diversified and the operating departments were in quite different fields, the Development department was forced into areas which were "even more speculative," taking on the riskiest, least related projects.

The typical venture launched by the Development department in the 1960's was described by one individual as a "large scale 'frontal assault' on a new market." A venture often consisted of several products aimed at the same market. Most often, these required heavy front end investment and when they ran into obstacles, the typical reaction was to "call another division in" and "pour more money in." The result was that when ventures failed, they were large scale failures, well into the tens of millions of dollars.

Relations with Other Departments

The ventures launched were "more or less fully self-contained" with large staffs of technical personnel and the venture's own facilities. The Development department's relations with operating departments were thus minimal.

Nevertheless, in the operating departments there was some dissatisfaction with the Development department's ventures in the sixties.

Some individuals felt that they lacked the people resources and close disciplined management and attention which were found in the operating departments.

As the ventures were self-contained they did not rely on other departments for assistance. There was little competition for resources as funds were not constrained. An individual in one of the operating departments explained:

> "Everybody has just about all the money they wanted for ventures. All the departments were encouraged to do new things. We were not competing with each other. Management didn't put an upper limit on what would be spent. If you had a good project, it was funded."

The Development department's interactions with the Central Reseach department were also minimal during the 1960's. This was attributed to the completely different orientations and objectives of the departments. The Central Research department conducted "academic, basic research." This orientation developed during the 1930's and 1940's when the operating departments grew to a size where they could support their own research organizations. As research pertinent to existing businesses was farmed out to the operating departments, Central Research became more "basic," pursuing projects of a much longer range nature.

During the sixties, the Assistant Director of the Development department felt that the skills in the Central Research department were not relevant to the task of his department. Thus, a new organization was built "from the ground up" within the Development department. It was observed that much of the money spent on the department's ventures really went into building this organization, serving to inflate the cost of these ventures. Although much smaller than Central Research, which was the largest research organization in the company, this department grew to be substantial in size.

MANAGEMENT PHILOSOPHY

The philosophy and atmosphere in the company that prevailed during this period shaped the venture activities. The dominating idea was an extreme confidence in the company's capabilities. This was reflected in the ventures in the following ways. There was great optimism in discussing ventures, "everything always looked good, problems were solvable, and the venture was always heading in the right direction." Second, there was a reluctance to recognize or accept that a venture could fail. Thus, when one ran into difficulty, the corporate response was to try to overcome the problem by committing additional resources. Third, it was believed that the time required to develop a venture into a large profitable business could be collapsed. This idea of reducing the time required to launch a venture was central to the "frontal assault" approach of the sixties.[1]

A fourth characteristic of the sixties was that the products developed were of the highest quality. One individual observed:

"We offered nothing but the best--no crass commercialization." It was felt that during the 60's several ventures priced themselves out of the market because of a tendency to resist compromise in product quality or performance even when economically warranted.

The Assistant Director of the Development department had almost total freedom in investigating new opportunities, determining the strategy for ventures, and guiding their operations. The degree of Executive Committee involvement was determined by the size of the venture and amount of funds it was consuming. The Assistant Director of the Development department observed:

> "The Executive Committee only closely watched a venture when it became a big consumer of capital. Capital was the trigger for their attention."

The Executive Committee established a Subcommittee on Planning composed of three vice presidents. They followed the ventures more closely than the total committee meeting with the Director or Assistant Director of the Development department every few weeks. The Development department reported on ventures formally to the full Executive Committee only quarterly. The Executive Committee rarely directed that a venture be discontinued. Instead it would provide that continuation of a venture was contingent on meeting certain established goals and targets.

GROWTH AND EVOLUTION

From 1960 to 1966, new venture activities were of increasing importance to the Development department and gradually took an increasing share of its time. The number of staff people working on ventures grew from twelve to over 200 people.

In 1966, the Director of the Development department retired and the Assistant Director was promoted to that position. The organization structure of the department was changed to reflect the increasing importance of its venture activities. These were carried out directly by the department director with the other department functions reporting to his assistant. The organization is shown in Figure 5-2.

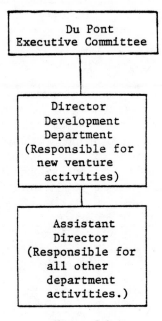

Figure 5-2

In 1968, the Director of the Development department was promoted to General Manager of an operating department. He was replaced by another individual who headed up the department for only one year before becoming an Assistant General Manager of an operating department.

In 1969, several large start-up ventures were being discontinued or spun off. These ventures had been initiated in the early sixties and had come through the pipeline in parallel. One successful venture had been transferred to an operating department. Successful and promising products in other ventures were beginning to be spun off to operating departments.

At the peak of DuPont's venturing activity, 25 "new ventures" were underway. The bulk of these were in the operating departments with only five in the Development department. By 1969, several of these had run up losses in the tens of millions of dollars and were being shut down. Minority equity positions in six small companies had been acquired under the "embryonic investment program" and in 1969, the company was making plans to divest these.

A member of the Executive Committee commented on the change in attitude toward ventures that occurred in about 1969:

"At no time was there a precipitous withdrawal of support ventures. No one woke up one day and said 'Let's not do it anymore.' It was a gradual thing and a variety of factors contributed to it."

New Business Opportunities Division: 1970-1976

CORPORATE SITUATION

In the late sixties, DuPont's corporate situation began to change. The general economic situation was becoming unfavorable due to rising inflation and in 1970, the first recession since the early 1960's.

DuPont's earnings had been in a downtrend since 1965. Many of the company's patents had expired resulting in overcapacity and pressure on prices. The Kennedy Round tariff cuts had hit the chemical industry particularly hard increasing foreign competition especially in textiles from the Far East. Sales in 1970 were down slightly from a year earlier and profits had declined by about 10%. In the decade 1960 to 1970 sales had increased by close to 60%, however, earnings had increased the first half of the decade and declined the second half, so that 1970 earnings were at a level equal to 1963's, and only about 20% higher than 1960. Although DuPont's balance sheet remained very strong, the company was entering a capital short period.

The outlook for the company's existing businesses was becoming more favorable. Its product portfolio included a larger percentage of new and growing businesses than a decade earlier. In the period 1960 to 1972, more than 50 new products (not including product modifications or improvements) had been introduced and in 1972 more than one-quarter of sales were from products less than 15 years old.

CORPORATE STRATEGY

The changing corporate situation brought about a shift in corporate strategy.

Corporate diversification slowed and the diversification of departments into related areas was given priority over corporate diversification into businesses farther afield. There was a basic change in the philosophy and atmosphere within the company.

A member of the Executive Committee explained:

"No one suddenly turned a valve on this. We are talking about degrees of emphasis."

This transition from a phase of expansion to one of consolidation is clearly reflected in the annual reports of 1969, 1970, and 1971 as shown below:

1969

"Newly developed products are expected to account for half of the company's earnings growth over the next five years...The company will continue to broaden its business base by entering new markets."

1970 Annual Report

"The long-term outlook remains excellent. The markets for chemical industry products are expanding with growth in physical volume expected to average 6% to 7% a year throughout the 70's. DuPont...is particularly strong in those products having high growth potential world wide...A number of new ventures which have been a drain on earnings are moving to the commercial phase...The company is making intensive efforts to improve profits by improving productivity and reducing costs. In 1970, economics were achieved through systematic company wide re-evaluation of activities and programs."

1971 Annual Report

"During the past two years the company has pursued a rigorous program to reduce costs and increase profitability. Manufacturing operations have been consolidated in several product areas. A number of unprofitable operations have been dropped... Our work force has been cut 10% during the last two years chiefly through normal attrition and reduced hiring. Major organizational changes have been made including an extensive realignment of product lines among industrial divisions to facilitate the development and marketing of related products."

RESEARCH POLICY

In about 1970, there was also a change in the direction of research and development. There was greater emphasis on research and development in support of the existing businesses through product improvement and product line extensions and a decline in "basic" or "pioneering" research. Thus, departmental research organizations were directed to support their existing products and channel their pioneering research to the Central Research department. Two factors influenced this. One was a shortage of funds and a desire to increase the return on dollars invested in research. The other factor was that the environment for research was getting tougher with increasing government regulation of new product introductions and longer lead times for their development. As its name implies, the research "establishment" at DuPont was not increased and decreased in size "with every pop in the business cycle." Rather, changes in corporate policy were reflected by shifting the focus of research efforts. Most important was the focus of the departmental research organizations which consumed approximately 90% of total research expenditures.

SUPPORT FOR VENTURES

Support for the company's venture activities diminished in the period 1969 to 1971. One major reason for this was the changing corporate situation and strategy. One member of the Executive Committee summed it up stating:

> "In a capital short period you clearly finance first those businesses you are already in. The urge to diversify is less. In fact, you simply don't diversify when you are short of capital unless your existing businesses are in trouble and ours were not."

The second factor bringing about a decline in support for venturing was the experience of the 60's. The five start-up ventures launched by the Development department had run up total pre-commercial costs of approximately $80 million, almost $50 million in one venture alone. And, this was only a fraction of the company-wide total.

The time frame of management's expectations contributed to the growing dissatisfaction with the performance of ventures. A member of the Development department explained:

> "Top management believed that you could develop a $50 million business in five to ten years if sufficient resources were committed. After a couple of years, it became apparent that we couldn't speed up new business development. Management became disillusioned with the progress of our ventures. The irony is that some of those ventures which looked so bad in 1969 turned out okay. We just expected results too soon."

In fact, one venture was a major success growing into a business with over $100 million in sales in 1976. A former Director of the Development department felt that this single venture justified the entire Development department program.

Attitudes towards new ventures (which ultimately affected the Development department) were influenced more by the ventures launched in the operating divisions than by those of the Development department. The operating departments were "where the action was."

Many in the operating departments felt that the company's overall ventures program was a failure.   The comments below were typical assessments:

> "It is awfully easy to launch diversification efforts in several attractive directions and build these up in scale but you incur a heck of a lot of expense before you get the first buck back. In the late 60's it became apparent that this could become pretty expensive and far reaching without the necessary management attention.   The Executive Committee got disenchanted with the concept."

> "There is nothing wrong with rolling the dice on a big venture if its obviously a winner, but if you roll them many times on those that are 'iffy,' and chew up money in chunks of $50 million at a crack that gets to be a bloody game. We did some of that in the 60's."

> "The experience of the 60's put a large damper on the concept that all you had to do is take off in twenty directions. Management became particularly disenchanted with $50 million and $100 million holes."

The third factor which brought a change in new venture policy in about 1970 was that many of the ventures launched were moving in parallel toward commercialization. This facilitated the winding down of the venture program since a large percentage of them could be disposed of either by being spun off to a division or being discontinued.

CREATION OF NBO

In 1970, the New Business Opportunities Division (NBO) was created within the Development department.   The decline of the Development department's venture activities had become evident in 1968 and 1969. The appointment of a new director of the department in 1969 was a key event because the individual selected favored a "MICRO" approach to launching ventures rather than that of the Development department. He implemented this new approach by creating the NBO. The manager who headed up the NBO observed:

> "There are several ways to change a department like the Development department.   If you have enough power, you can modify its formal charter, or an alternative is to destroy it and build a new department. The new Development department director didn't have the kind of power to achieve the former. So he started up the NBO and let the Development department's old venture program die out."

The decline of DuPont's venture program could have resulted in the Development department simply being disbanded. However, instead it was reduced in scope and carried out on a smaller scale with a different approach. The decision to continue the new venture division function on a smaller scale rather than discontinuing it was attributed to two factors. First, DuPont's culture highly valued research based new ventures. Historically these accounted for most of the company's leading products. Thus, there was a reluctance to completely discontinue this activity. A member of the Executive Committee explained:

> "We are a research based company. Our most profitable products were developed from research. Thus, we always want a stable of ventures. We try to keep it appropriately sized for our business situation."

The second factor was that DuPont was conservatively managed financially. The company had minimal long term debt and did not "spend up to the peg." Thus, it could "suffer for a couple of years" while adjusting the level of its venture activities to the appropriate size.

CHANGE IN PHILOSOPHY

The approach and philosophy of the NBO represented almost a complete reversal from that of the Development department in the 60's. The Director of the Development department who established the NBO commented on this change in orientation:

> "The NBO evolved as a change in organization within the Development department, but the significant change was in its way of carrying out new business development. This change in approach resulted from our disappointing experience in the 1960's.
>
> 'The approach we adopted puts more emphasis on finding a way to run a meaningful market test at an earlier stage while trying to concentrate on not making any significant early capital investment. We believe it is possible to be innovative in using equipment and facilities which already exist in the company. Our objective is to try to sell a product (which is the only true measure of value) before asking for any sizable commitment of funds."

The controller of the Development department also discussed this change in philosophy:

"In the fifteen years I have been here, our philosophy has changed markedly. In the early sixties, we had a big block of ventures in which we came out with several major products aimed at the same market. These did not really materialize as quickly or easily as we had expected. We now attempt to make a venture largely self-supporting early on. We don't invest a large amount of money in a venture until there are indications of market acceptance and evidence of a financial return. This more recent approach appears to be more successful. If I had to say why, I would say because when you simultaneously launch several products you don't really know whether the market needs them. In our present approach, we live with the market for a while and then decide what additional needs we can fill."

The manager of the NBO observed that there was a clear business justification for the NBO approach versus that of the sixties:

"When we learned that new ventures take a much longer time to develop, it made us rethink our approach. If it takes 20 years instead of 10 for a venture to develop, you have to be more careful how you spend your money and more selective about opportunities to pursue. The time-value of money has become a more important consideration and we have thus sought to get a positive cash flow as early as possible."

There were five main aspects of the approach taken by the NBO which differed from that of the Development department in the 60's.

RESYNTHESES OF RESOURCES AND CAPABILITIES

The NBO sought ventures which were more closely related to the company's existing resources and capabilities. They sought ventures which were less risky and "far out." The department director explained this as follows:

"One of the things we do in a very disciplined manner is to look five or ten years down the road and say to ourselves 'suppose this venture turns out to be successful--what will it look like then, and what are all the resources we would need to get from here to there?' Then we ask, 'Of all of these required resources, which do DuPont already have?' I believe that we are better off leading from some strength. If we have few or none of the necessary resources and other companies have them, it would be difficult to convince me to undertake the venture. This says something about the degree of diversification I am willing to support. There are innumerable opportunities we can pursue. I give those that we have the resources for highest priority."

Thus, the NBO sought to develop ventures which represented recombinations or resyntheses of existing company resources and capabilities.

RELATIONS WITH OTHER DEPARTMENTS

The second major difference was that while the ventures of the 60's were essentially self-contained, the NBO sought to have lean low-budget ventures which drew heavily, either formally or informally, on the people and other resources of the various operating departments. The NBO manager explained:

"Our job is basically to identify the resources that are needed for a venture, determine whether DuPont has these resources in house, or at least enough of them to be successful, and then to pull them together and try to manage them. This differs from our role during the 1960's. Then, we would have tried to create those same resources ourselves.

You do better when the business you're aiming at is close to what you already know. My job then becomes to organize and to tap the necessary resources to test our assumptions and to carry out that plan."

For example, in one venture which involved developing a device to aid textile designers, researchers in the Photo Products department worked on applying a technology for reproducing colors which existed in that department while an individual in the Fibers department surveyed the potential market for the device.

BEACHHEAD VENTURES

A third difference in approach was that the NBO attempted to launch small ventures targeted at a particular market niche as compared to the "frontal assault" ventures of the 60's in which a broader market was attacked with several parallel product introductions. The five ventures launched during the sixties had precommercial costs averaging almost ten times the average for the six ventures launched by the NBO. The latter averaged under $2 million. In the approach adopted by the NBO, the notion of "testing" is the key. The manager of the NBO stated:

"Our entry strategy is to try to develop a 'beach head'--an approach that will give us a niche in the market place. Our aim is to make money in establishing that niche. The first step is to test out all of the assumptions with regard to our resource base and the niche we're aiming at. Many times those assumptions are incorrect, but we have the flexibility to make changes. Nevertheless, ultimately it may turn out that the niche is not a business."

This approach is clearly intended to avoid the large scale failures that were experienced in the sixties.

LONG TERM IMPACT

The fourth major difference was that the mission of the NBO was not to redirect DuPont or make a substantial short-term impact on its diversity, but to establish financially sound businesses in future growth markets. An important element of this approach was to defer major financial commitments until the new business was proven.

Although ventures were initially small, the NBO still had the objective of impacting on the company. The critical difference from the approach of the sixties was the time frame considered. The NBO did not expect its ventures to have a major impact for at least 15 or 20 years.

The Director of the Development department also felt that it would be unrealistic to attempt to significantly increase the product market diversity of DuPont. There were few markets that DuPont did not sell to in one way or another and even though it was a chemical company, its diversity in terms of products and markets was comparable to that of a conglomerate.

An individual in one of the operating departments had the following comment about the role of the NBO:

"The NBO is one of the charming things we have around. It is a nice luxury but, the NBO is not DuPont. It's a nice little organization but in DuPont the real action is in the operating departments, even in new product development. The NBO only takes what does not fit into a department or what they can generate themselves."

LEARNING PHILOSOPHY

The fifth difference between the Development department of the 60's and the NBO of the 70's was one of philosophy. In the 60's, ventures were seen as "the implementation of a plan" for entry into new markets. Venture strategies were adapted and modified when they ran into difficulty but the inclination was to attempt to overcome the problems encountered by committing additional resources. In contrast, the NBO's philosophy was to "learn and adapt." The idea was to test business ideas and modify them in response to the feedback from the experiments carried out. The terms "success" and "failure" which were appropriate for the approach of the 60's were considered inappropriate when applied to the NBO's ventures. The NBO manager explained:

> "Success and failure are terms which bother me. I do not think they are appropriate for what we do. For example, two of our ventures, Cronel and Viaflow had similar objectives: to develop a technology into a product, develop a plan to test market that product, and get the test market results. The test market results in Viaflow were that people were buying. In Cronel people weren't buying. From my perspective, we ran two experiments and got different answers. It's like trying to decide between investing in the stocks of two companies. If you investigate both and you decide not to buy one, you haven't 'failed'."

Organization

The oranization structure of the department in 1970 is shown in Figure 5-3.

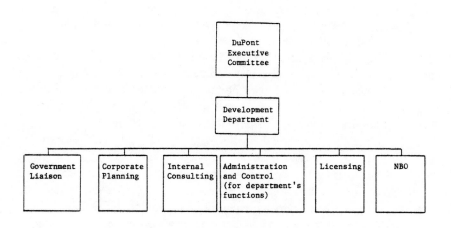

Figure 5-3

The activities of the Development department included corporate planning, internal consulting, licensing technology which was not used internally, the accounting and control functions for the department, and the NBO.

The licensing manager interfaced closely with the NBO. When new opportunities arose, the decision had to be made whether to pursue it internally or license it. When a venture failed, the licensing manager would often become involved and attempt to license what had been developed.

The organization of the NBO itself was described as very fluid. It changed to meet the needs of the individual projects and ventures at a particular point in time. The group responsible for searching out new ventures and screening ideas varied in size from year to year and its activity ranged from "almost dormant" to "very active." The activity of this group depended to a large extent on the amount of money the Executive Committee appropriated.

The individuals in that group were very mobile, and when a venture idea was approved, the individual who studied it initially often moved out of this group to run the venture. He might not be replaced for a long period of time, but then several individuals would be added to this group and the cycle begun again.

STAFFING

The individual chosen to head up the NBO had begun his career at DuPont in the Plastics department twelve years earlier. He had spent three years in reseach in another department and then nine in sales and marketing before coming to the NBO.

Most of the individuals in the NBO had technical backgrounds and many had worked on the Development department ventures during the prior decade. One member of the department described a typical individual within the NBO as "someone with commercial savvy and a background from different departments in the company."

Generally, individuals who came into the NBO from an operating department followed one of three paths. After a few years, they either returned to a new position in an operating department, returned to an operating department as part of a venture that was spun off from the NBO, or remained permanently in the NBO. In 1974, a decision was made to hire MBAs into the NBO as one of the entry level positions in DuPont. The rationale for this was that it would give them an opportunity to get a relatively quick, broad overview of the company before they were offered employment in an operating department. In their work with the NBO, their lack of contacts in DuPont was considered a disadvantage, but this was partly overcome by their use of the more experienced, long-time DuPont people in the NBO to facilitate access to other departments.

NBO APPROACH

The NBO's activities were limited to start-up ventures. The department evaluated potential new business ideas that were generated both within DuPont and outside of it. When an outside party came to DuPont with a venture idea, the host department would contact the NBO if the idea did not fit into an operating department. The key factor in determining who would develop a venture was where the required resources were located.

The NBO did not carry out any internal idea generating or brainstorming, but rather served as a clearing house for the ideas of others.

When a potential venture was brought to the attention of the NBO, it was evaluated by a committee of several department members, usually including the manager. If a decision was made to pursue the opportunity, two individuals were usually assigned to manage the initial phase of the venture. This gave the NBO manager flexibility in choosing a Venture Manager. Usually within a year one of these individuals was selected as the Venture Manager.

One of the first responsibilities of the Venture Manager was to prepare a business plan. The Development department director stressed the importance of planning:

> "Our aim is to shorten the time and dollars necessary to get a true market appraisal of a potential new business. To achieve this, we put a great deal of emphasis on well thought out planning and accurate estimation of financial costs."

The business plan was updated as the venture went along and more information was gained. There was no pressure on a Venture Manager to adhere an earlier plan if he had gained information which warranted changing it.

RESOURCE BOARD

Early in a venture, a "Resource Board" was established. Members of other departments who could contribute to the business were asked to serve on this board, usually aside one or two members of the NBO and its manager. The Resource Board was viewed as a prestigious appointment--"it gave the NBO an opportunity to cater to their egos somewhat" and build support. The purposes of the Resource Board were to assess the progress of the venture, make suggestions and recommendations, to facilitate communication and cooperation with other departments in the company, and to plan for the ultimate disposition of the venture. The Development department director discussed the rationale for having a board for each of the ventures:

> "Resource Boards are working boards of people who can contribute and have access to the required resources in the operating departments. One of the things I feel strongly about is that it would be a mistake to try to build completely self-contained venture groups in this department. You lose a lot by transferring a person out of his department to this venture. When you contract out development work to other departments, you get not only the expertise of the individual who works on it, but also the help of his supervisor and others around him. The Resource Board compensates in some way for not having a completely self-sufficient venture group, and it gives us access to greater resources."

A former board member discussed what he saw as its function:

> "The role of the Resource Board is to provide the varied inputs that the Venture Manager needs to round out his experience. Its members operate both as individual specialists and as a group to support, criticize or modify the Venture Manager's proposals. The Resource Board provides a sounding board for the Venture Manager. To a large degree, this is the way DuPont manages its businesses. We like to get all points of view. Very few decisions in DuPont are made unilaterally."

When the venture was spun off to an operating department, the Resource Board was usually disbanded.

MANAGEMENT CONTROL

A Venture Manager reported to the Resource Board quarterly. He determined the nature of the reports he would provide to both the Resource Board and the manager of the NBO. The only required report was a monthly budget for the year for all expense and revenue categories.

The relationship between the NBO manager and the venture managers was likened to that of a venture capitalist and the entrepreneurs he had invested in. It was generally observed that the NBO manager served more of an advisory role than a decision making role with respect to the ventures.

In contrast to the approach of the 1960's the initial objectives for a venture were limited. They were often stated in terms of questions that the Venture Manager would attempt to answer, knowledge that he would attempt to gain, and the activities that would be carried out towards these ends.

The Controller for the Development department contrasted tracking the performance of ventures to that of on-going businesses:

> "In your existing businesses you evaluate return on investment. We do not attempt to evaluate return on investment for ventures because normally we haven't invested much. We will use someone else's plant, equipment and what have you at least to the point where the venture is a viable business. We are more concerned that the venture is going toward a profitable operating position and that we are achieving it within our budget constraints.
>
> With a venture you have to go beyond the bottom line because very often it hasn't developed to a point where there is anything even close to a profit. In fact, losses may be increasing and the venture may still be healthy as long as you have a picture that it will turn profitable and you'll get a good return."

The Controller's staff did the accounting for individual ventures. Individuals from his staff were assigned to specific ventures and reported on a "very heavy" dotted line to the Venture Manager. They developed an accounting and information system for their venture and reported to the Development department controller at least monthly on the progress on the venture. These were typical accounting reports with sales, expenses, and profits versus budget and explanations for variances. These reports did not go to the Resource Board, because a venture's performance varied widely from month to month.

The monthly accounting reports were distributed to the Manager of the NBO and the Director of the Development Department. However, the Director of the Development Department did not get involved in the details of individual ventures. He explained:

> "I intentionally try not to get into the substantive details of a venture. I like to understand them, but I feel it is critical to have the decisions made at the level of the Venture Manager. My job is to set the proper environment, decide on the type of approach we will take and assure that the right people will run the ventures. I am here to have ideas bounced off of and give the Venture Managers authority and control over the ventures. My responsibility to top management is to control the money and to know how we are progressing."

The Development Department reported to a "liaison" Vice President on the Executive Committee. He had a fairly detailed knowledge of the ventures. The rest of the Executive Committee received an annual plan for the whole department including the NBO and individual ventures, as well as quarterly reports. However, they were primarily interested in the "direction" individual ventures were going in and what the total cost of the NBO was.

In general, there was a lower level of Executive Committee attention devoted to individual ventures of the NBO than those of the Development department in the sixties. This was attributed to the smaller size of the ventures. The NBO manager felt that this gave the venture group flexibility:

> "There is little resistance to redefining a venture's strategy if the argument makes sense. A low profile is important because you don't have to continually answer to people who don't know what you're doing. The other reason is that it takes a lot of time and energy to have a high profile, and that energy should be spent carrying out the objectives of the venture.
>
> If you've got a high profile, it is harder to change your approach-- the organization becomes committed to that approach and there is resistance to changing the plan. Exposure to the organization produces commitment to an approach and that is difficult to reverse. We have tried to structure the organization so that there are as few bosses to go through as possible. My boss (head of the Development department) reports to the Executive Committee. There isn't much space between the guys who head the ventures and the top."

The decision to discontinue a venture was made by either the NBO manager or the Venture Manager. Individuals higher up in the organization generally did not get involved. This was in contrast to the sixties when the Executive Committee was sometimes instrumental in the decision to discontinue a venture. The NBO manager stated that if he felt a venture should be continued, the Development department director will usually "let it run." The same attitude prevailed in the relationship between the NBO manager and the Venture manager. The former would sometimes let a venture run for several months after he felt that it should be discontinued so that the decision would come from the Venture Manager.

When a venture was "discontinued" it was not a large scale failure as in the sixties but only the beginning of another phase in its development. It would come under the jurisdiction of the Licensing Manager who would attempt to find opportunities for other companies which were either in a different direction or on a different scale.

"The word 'salvage' might describe my role, but it has the wrong connotation. It implies something of little value when very often a situation I am attempting to license represents an excellent business opportunity for someone else."

For most ventures there was usually a successful business that could be salvaged.

VENTURE SPIN-OFF

A venture which was "successful" was transferred out of the NBO when its potential had been determined. The actual timing depended on subjective factors such as the individuals involved, the progress of the business, and the organizational fit in its new home. The transfer of a business to an operating department was often a difficult step and one NBO member pointed out:

"If you were truly looking for new businesses and new markets, then by definition there is no easy fit with an existing DuPont department."

There appeared to be little desire within the NBO to retain profitable ventures. One department member explained:

"Success for us is in placing the ventures. That is our ultimate goal--to have somebody want the venture--to demonstrate enough potential, profitability or whatever so that someone wants it. There is no doubt about the genuine satisfaction that people get in seeing a venture placed. well. There would be reluctance to give a venture up if it was going to the wrong place, but that's not usually a problem. From the very beginning, we're planning for the ultimate placement of the business."

One of the functions of the Resource Board was to plan for a smooth transfer of the venture of the NBO to an operating department. The individuals from the operating department who had served on the Resource Board had been with the venture through its growing pains. Thus they were able to give their management an inside view of what it was. This facilitated a smooth transfer of the venture and reduced the possibility of conflict afterwards.

The Director of the Development department seemed to have little desire to retain ventures after they were commercialized. He seemed to prefer the initiation of ventures to "empire building." He commented:

"We hope that ventures will move to an industrial department when their feasibility has been tested. We don't want to become an industrial department by retaining ventures because it is not our charter. We would lose our ability to start new ones if that happened. The best way to ensure that the transfer is made smoothly is to have an industrial department involved in a working way from the beginning on the Resource Board or otherwise."

The head of the NBO also shared these views. He stated:

"The only thing that is certain is that a successful venture will leave this department--because the business of this department is to start new ones. If we continue to run old ones, then we will cease to start new ones. The only time it bothers me to turn over a venture to an operating department is when it is done before our objectives have been realized. Then if the thing doesn't succeed, it reflects on me and the NBO. The pressure to turn it over is greatest when there is a close fit with an operating department. There have even been some ventures identified here, where the conclusion has been that all the resources reside somewhere else and they have been immediately turned over to the proper department."

1975 REORGANIZATION

In 1975, there was a major change in the organization of the Development department. It was combined with Central research into a single department. Several of its functions including internal management consulting, serving as the Executive Committee's staff arm and Corporate Planning were placed elsewhere in the company where top management felt they would be better served. The historical mission--serving as the staff arm of the Executive Committee--was assigned to a new department called Corporate Planning. This was attributed to the reluctance of the Executive Committee to really use the Development department as its staff arm in recent yeas. The change in organization is shown in Figure 5-4.

In 1976, the NBO manager was promoted to Director of the Development division. Prior to that the Assistant Director of the Central Research and Development Department had held both titles. The effect of this promotion was to have the Development division assume the functions of the NBO.

RELATIONS WITH CENTRAL RESEARCH

The combination of the Central Research and Development department brought about some degree of increased coordination and cooperation between the two departments. This had been an objective

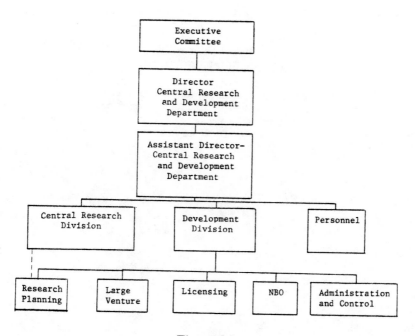

Figure 5-4

since the creation of the NBO. An integral part of the philosophy was to attempt to use the existing corporate resources rather than duplicating them in the department.

One of the NBO manager's first responsibilities was to begin working more closely with Central Research. Since the two departments had different objectives and orientations, there was limited overlap.

In 1975 reorganization and changes which accompanied it facilitated cooperation and coordination between the Research and NBO departments in several ways including the following:

1. The Directors of the NBO and Research were peers, reporting to the same individual. They dealt with each other directly rather than through intermediaries.

2. Both individuals were on the Research and Development department staff. This body, composed of eight key individuals in the R & D department, met formally at least once per month.

3. A Research Planning Group which previously was in the Research division, was transferred to the Development division. This group of twelve people helped the Research division evaluate research projects in terms of their business potential before they were initiated.   Its role, however, was strictly advisory.

CONTINUED EVOLUTION

In considering the future of new venture activities in DuPont, a member of the Executive Committee observed:

"The changes in our new venture activities are not irreversible. Our approach will change as the intermediate term business outlook does. We could start up large scale ventures again like we did a decade ago.   Even though that may be ill advised, all we need is extra money to get into the bad habits of the sixties."

NOTES

[1]It ultimately became apparent that although product development could be accelerated, market acceptance of truly innovative products often could not be predicted or speeded up.

CHAPTER 6

RALSTON PURINA NEW VENTURE DIVISION

Evolution from 1967 to 1976

The New Venture Division at Ralston Purina was established in September 1967. At that time, the company incorporated the following four major product areas, all of which involved food or animal feed:

1. "Chow" products - over 100 basic rations of animal feed for livestock, poultry and other animals.
2. Grocery products -the largest and fastest growing grocery products were pet foods, mainly Purina Dog Chow and Cat Chow. This product area also included "Chex" cereals and snack items.
3. Seafood - the Van Camp division acquired in the early '60s was the country's largest tuna producer (marketing under the "Chicken of the Sea" label), and sold other seafood products as well.
4. Poultry products - the company operated 49 poultry processing plants, byproduct plants, and hatcheries.

The common threads that linked Ralston Purina's businesses were protein and nutrition. The 1967 annual report stated:

> In broad terms, the business of Ralston Purina Company revolves around the vital area of protein industries. Approximately half of the company's business is represented in the manufacturing and marketing of feeds and feed supplements for livestock, poultry, and other animals and fowl.... The company also processes some 55 million bushels of soybeans annually... a principal protein source for the company's livestock and poultry feeds. Another important area of operation is the production, processing, and marketing of protein foods from both the land and sea.

Ralston Purina was organized into seven divisions. In addition to four divisions corresponding to the product areas listed above, there was a Corporate staff, an International Division, producing and marketing the company's products abroad, and a Purchasing Division which operated 8 soybean processing facilities.

In 1967, the company earned $30 million on sales of $1.3 billion. During the previous decade, sales had more than doubled, increasing each year. Profits had increased from $19 million in 1958 to a high of $45 million in 1966 before declining in 1967. (See Appendices 6-1 and 6-2 for financial summary.)

The financial position of the company was strong. Management traditionally had been financially conservative, maintaining an A bond rating and a debt/total capitalization ratio of less than 25%. Anticipating major growth in the immediate future, $40 million of debentures were issued in December 1967 and shareholder authorization for the creation of 6 million shares of preferred stock was obtained.

When the New Venture Division was established, the company was undergoing a period a major transition. The changes taking place can be best understood in a historical context.

Company History

The company was founded by William Danforth in 1894. His personal philosophy, which emphasized the full development of the individual and "Christain leadership," shaped the dominant values of the company. Even in 1976, two decades after his death, these values were reflected in Ralston's Corporate Objectives. (See Appendix 6-3.)

From its founding through the 1950s, Ralston Purina was mainly a livestock and poultry feed company and the "Chow" business clearly dominated the company. However, in 1957, Purina Dog Chow was introduced and quickly became the nation's largest selling dry dog food. The pet food business grew rapidly during the next decade and by 1967, it was challenging the traditional dominance of the Chow Division. One manager summed up the changes that this brought, stating: "During the sixties we began the transition from a production-oriented feed producer to a marketing-oriented diversified company."

SITUATION IN 1967

In 1967, the Danforth family was relinquishing financial control of Ralston. Five years earlier, the family had decided to list the stock on the New York Stock Exchange and it was becoming more widely held. Between 1962 and 1967, the number of stockholders doubled. In 1967, the Danforth family still controlled approximately 20% of the outstanding stock. However, by 1971 most of this stock was sold and the transition toward public ownership was almost complete.

During the sixties, there was a parallel transition away from family management. In 1963, the first non-Danforth chief executive took office. Gradually during the next decade, family members left active management with the last family member leaving his position as Vice President of the Chow Division in 1972.

During 1967 and 1968, major changes were being made in top management and on the Board of Directors. In those two years, seven new members were added to the Board. Hal Dean followed Raymond

Rowland as Chairman, Albert O'Brien moved up from Executive Vice President to President, and three Corporate Vice Presidents were appointed Executive Vice Presidents.

The dominant figure in bringing about this transition in Ralston Purina was Hal Dean. He became President and Chief Operating Officer in 1964 and four years later advanced to Chairman, President, and Chief Executive Officer.

In the first few years after becoming President he initiated a decentralization of Ralston's functional organization. However, he saw this as a part of a broader attempt to bring about a more fundamental change in the company. When Hal Dean took over as President, the company was somewhat bureaucratic. Although the consumer products area was emerging in the early sixties, the existing management saw the company primarily as the Chow Division. Hal Dean commented:

> I was attempting not only to decentralize, but to generate new thought processes - to change in a very basic way the type of company we were. But there was resistance. The increasing sophistication of our management has been a gradual process, a learning curve that the company has moved along for the last decade.

During the latter half of the sixties, Hal Dean was pushing for growth and diversification and taking an active part in operations. He was consolidating his position, putting people in whom he had confidence in key positions and molding the organization into a new form. This period of transition was characterized by some short-lived uncertainty as to whether the company's future direction was appropriate. This transition served to temporarily divert Hal Dean's energy away from the NVD.

ESTABLISHMENT OF THE NVD

In 1967, Hal Dean proposed the establishment of the New Venture Division. He was its initial sponsor and played a critical role in its later development. There were several reasons for setting up the New Venture Division.

Ralston Purina was considered a growth company. Its stock was valued at an above-average earnings multiple and top management sought rapid growth - 10-15% per year. The company was diversifying yet its portfolio of businesses consisted too heavily of mature or maturing businesses.

The "Chow" business was mature, not expected to grow faster than the economy as a whole. The poultry business was also seen to have limited growth potential.

The consumer products business - mainly pet food - was seen as the major growth area. Cat food was a new product which would be a source of increased sales in Consumer Products, however, Purina Dog Chow was ten years old and expected to succumb to the life cycle within a few years.[1] Looking for the future, there were no major new growth businesses on the horizon for the late seventies and beyond.

There was little likelihood that new businesses would emerge from the operating divisions. The divisions' main focus in new product development was on product line extensions - new products rather than new businesses. One result of the divisionalization and decentralization was that with the empha·is on divisional profit performance, some long-term new business development activities were lost in the pressures of day-to-day operations. Another consequence of divisionalization was that new business opportunities did not necessarily fit an existing division. For example, the soy-protein operation which appeared to some as having great potential fell between divisional lines. Although for several years, this had been seen as a potential long term opportunity, there was little impetus behind its development.

A third factor which some individuals felt played a role in the establishment of the New Venture Division was Hal Dean's orientation and management style. He was entrepreneurial, ambitious, hard-driving and growth oriented.

STAFFING

The individual selected to head up the New Venture Division was Win Golden, who had been the divisional Vice President - Protein, in the Purchasing Division. He was considered "somewhat of a maverick in the organization but well-respected."

He had had a close relationship with Hal Dean for several years and he had followed him up the corporate ladder through the Commodity Buying department. He had "done the circuit" including plant operations and commodity buying.

The Commodity Buying area had traditionally served as a "seedbed" for top management. It was a function of critical importance in the company because of the wide fluctuations in raw material prices and their impact on profit margins. Hal Dean had come up through this area as had an Executive Vice President under him and at one point prior to his tenure, the President, Executive Vice President, and two top people below them had advanced through the department. Hal Dean discussed the type of manager who typically came out of the Commodity Buying Department:

The commodity buyer develops a respect for the volatility of prices and an outstanding ability to analyze, synthesize and make a decision. The job requires you to learn about and analyze all the things that will affect price trends, take this tremendous variety of fact and uncertainty and make a decision.

He felt these were important qualities for top managers in Ralston Purina.

Prior to being selected to head up the New Venture Division, Win Golden had also worked part-time on special projects for Hal Dean. His most recent one was a review of corporate Research and Development policy. In his report on this, he had pointed to the need for a more systematized and programmed research effort including expanded protein research. This project gave him contacts in the R&D area, and an understanding of protein technology, which were valuable in the later operations of the New Venture Division.

In 1967, Win Golden was preparing to leave Ralston Purina and had made his intentions known to Hal Dean. He saw the company developing into two bureaucratic divisions (the Chow Division and Consumer Products) and saw little future for himself in the type of organization that seemed to be developing. Hal Dean offered the New Venture Division to him as a chance to step outside the normal structure. Several times after that, Hal Dean similarly used the New Venture Division to hold others like Win Golden who were becoming dissatisfied with the climate in the company.

ORGANIZATION AND MISSION

Win Golden was given the title of Director, New Venture Management in August 1967. He reported directly to Hal Dean, at that time President and Chief Operating Officer. The purpose of having the NVD report directly to the President was twofold. First, it would afford protection - it was less likely to be challenged or undermined - and it would facilitate access to corporate resources both in staff departments and in the operating divisions. It was planned that the NVD would operate as a cost center rather than having to be justified as a profit center and to limit its costs it would use existing internal resources as much as possible. Secondly, Hal Dean wanted to be closely involved with the ventures early in the idea development stage. He gave Win Golden feedback early in the development of his proposals. This avoided "having a lot of people spinning their wheels on ideas that we weren't interested in." Hal Dean's early involvement in ventures also resulted in his assuming more of a sponsor's role when these ventures came before the Budget Comittee.

NVD CHARTER

When set in 1967, the mission of the New Venture Division was rather broad. A press release issued announcing the establishment of the NVD stated:

> Mr. Golden's responsibilities in the area of New Venture Division Mangement wil encompass the direction and management of certain company acquisitions. He will also fill a coordination and liason role with all company divisions in the development and marketing of new products.

The NVD's intended mission was clarified by the end of 1967 when Win Golden wrote a charter detailing the NVD's objectives, authority and organization. This was presented to top management and approved in early 1968.

In the charter, he stated that the purpose of the NVD would be to "generate new business activity through internal development and acquisition that will expand the company's profitability and growth..." Its activities would be aimed toward "innovative breakthroughs into new businesses - not just to make minor renovations typically associated with new products."

The new businesses developed by the NVD would include any one or combination of the following:

1. A new product or line of products
2. Unique manufacturing or fabrication processes
3. Marketing innovations
4. Sales of services
5. Licensing of technology.

Additional objectives of the NVD were to train and develop managers and prepare them for broader corporate responsibility and to test the project management organization and evaluate its potential for other corporation activities.

The criteria established for venture projects were that they demonstrate the potential of the following:

1. Meeting or exceeding current corporate ROA guidelines.
2. Contributing pre-tax profits at an annual rate of $2 million within the fourth year of commercialization.
3. A growth in pre-tax profit of 16% compounded annually following the fourth year of commercialization.

4. Returning all research, engineering, development, and prestart-up expenses within the fourth year of commercialization.
5. Ten-year life expectancy from the point of commitment.

It was anticipated that the NVD could generate two ventures every three-year period which would meet the minimum financial objectives and one venture every five years which would have profit potential of twice the minimum objective.

It should be emphasized that the NVD was initially seen as a permanent department which would remain relatively small and have as its on-going mission the continual generation of new business activities. These would remain in the NVD at most, five years before being spun-off, either to an existing operating division of the company, as a new division, or merchandised as a divestment. There was no provision for or expectation that the NVD would retain any ventures indefinitely.

The process by which ventures develop was expected to follow six steps:

1. <u>Search and Identification</u> - this would involve a systematic scanning of the marketplace for unmet needs as well as review and monitoring of in-house resources (R&D, marketing, engineering) to solicit innovative ideas.
2. <u>Screening and Selection</u> - this would seek to evaluate objectively risks and potential of venture ideas.
3. <u>Feasibility and Concept Refinement</u> - this would involve low-level expenditures to refine the concept and position the venture.
4. <u>Concept Testing and Evaluation</u> - higher levels of expenditures would be required to test the viability of the venture and further define it.
5. <u>Commitment</u> - a finalized program with a hard financial profile and three- to five-year projection would be presented.
6. <u>Implementation</u> - a project team would be formalized to carry out the venture plan.

The planned organization structure of the NVD is shown in Figure 6-1. It was expected that in time additional project managers would be added.

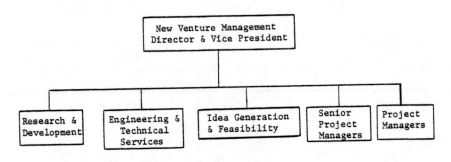

Figure 6-1

POTENTIAL CONFLICTS

The charter also identified several areas in which conflicts might develop with other divisions and recommended how these might be resolved or avoided.

Three areas identified were:

1. The initiation of ventures in competition with a division of the company. It was recommended that top management review at an early stage successfully screened projects with this in mind.

2. Drawing on divisions for required personnel. It was recommended that these resources be made available to the NVD through agreement with the operating division head.

3. The third potential area of conflict was in the timing of the spin-off of ventures. In discussing this, the charter stated:

There can be no set formula for determining either the recipient or the exact timing of a venture spin-off. Some ventures will logically and conveniently move into operating areas faster than others. Often raw concepts which may be uncovered in the normal New Venture searching pattern may be given divisional exposure almost immediately following identification. More complex ventures may require development and operational experience for a three- to five-year period prior to spin-off.

Each venture will possess critically different considerations which must be objectively measured prior to spin-off if venture viability is to be maintained for the present and maximized for the future.

POLICY RECOMMENDATIONS: Normally it will be the responsibility of New Venture Management to recommend and program the timing and the recipient of "spin-offs." If there should be disagreement or conflict concerning this normal process, it is recommended that top management, after a thorough review of all considerations, render the final judgment in each case."

STRATEGY PURSUED

In actuality, the activities of the New Venture Division differed from those outlined in the charter.

Hal Dean and Win Golden together developed a strategy for the NVD. Hal Dean's early instructions to Win Golden were: "Pay your own way." Hal Dean wanted Win Golden to proceed "prudently and cautiously" evaluating risk and potential return at each step of the way. His challenge to "pay his own way" placed demands on Win Golden. It was intended to force him to watch closely how he spent money and to avoid wastefulness.

In addition, it was felt resistance to the establishment of the NVD would be minimized and it would have the greatest chance for the support of the whole company if it maintained a low profile and did not become a cash drain. The NVD was not universally accepted throughout the company. Win Golden recognized the political importance of a low profile and a "pay as you go" approach and these served as key guidelines in his planning.

Even as he was writing the charter, outlining the long-term objectives of the NVD - to develop innovative, high potential businesses - Win Golden recognized that a quite different short-term strategy would be required to enable him to carry out this mission. Thus, the early efforts of the NVD were aimed at developing new businesses with quick cash payout that could be "cash cows" to support the longer-term innovative product developments which would require several years of high investments with an uncertain return. In setting up the NVD, top management had this strategy in mind and gave the NVD an initial "dowry" - a rather modest corporate expense budget and a plant producing soy proteins which Win Golden brought with him to the NVD. Win Golden explained that he was expected to become profitable almost from the first day of operations:

Hal told me that he wanted the corporate "dowry" to be as small as possible. You have to realize how "gutsy" it was to set up a department like this in what was still in many ways a very conservative company. If we had come in with a three or four million dollar loss in our first year, Hal would have gone to the mat for us, but he didn't want to have to do that. He was involved in other problems which were more important. If we had been given unlimited funds and a charter to make as much of an impact as possible in 10 years we would have operated differently. But the reality was that we were expected to pay our own way.

EARLY PERCEPTION OF NVD

Initially and through its first several years, the NVD was viewed in the company as a relatively insignificant activity. It was not expected to make a major impact on earnings and as one manager commented: "It was tolerated because it was small, the amount of damage it could do was minimal and it was a special interest of the chairman."

For Win Golden, taking charge of the NVD was a high risk move which was considered to be of questionable wisdom by many of his peers. When he took the job, he received "sympathy cards from most of my friends" expressing regret and misgivings for the future. He was stepping out of the mainstream of corporate advancement. He commented:

> Several people thought I was joining a losing effort. I was banking my future on Hal Dean's future desire and ability to support the NVD.

Evolution of the NVD

The evolution of the NVD from its origin in 1967 will be described in four sections below which reflect different phases in its development.

1967-1970

The NVD's first year was described as one of mainly "trouble-shooting" - assisting Hal Dean in a search for acquisitions and attempting to find alternative uses or buyers for plants which were unprofitable or underutilized.

Ralston Purina's acquisition activities during this period were carried out mainly by Hal Dean, a few staff members who assisted him and the NVD. During 1967 and 1968 their main focus was on fast food restaurant chains. The NVD played a minor role in the implementation of the fast food acquisition which fell through. Shortly thereafter discussions began with Foodmaker and it was acquired in March 1968.

The NVD worked on this acquisition as well as its subsequent integration into Ralston Purina. The main acquisition search efforts of the NVD were very brief - only undertaken until the other activities could get underway.

Attempts to find alternative uses for underutilized plants was the other early activity of the NVD. In 1967-1969, two plants were focused on - the protein plant which reported to Win Golden when he was in the Purchasing Division and came with him to the NVD and a poultry processing plant in Wellston, Ohio.

INDUSTRIAL PROTEIN

Win Golden was very familiar with the protein plant (which produced primarily industrial protein) and had thought for several years that it could be a much larger and more profitable operation. The company's strategy in industrial protein was to produce the highest quality product which was feasible. Win Golden felt that pricing policies were unsound and they were producing better quality than was demanded by certain market segments. He had been overridden by his superior in the Purchasing Division on this issue. Hal Dean felt this business was misplaced in the Purchasing Division and when the NVD was set up, the protein plant was transferred to it. Shifting the business to the NVD was intended to change its orientation from the bulk/commodity/production ethic that dominated in the Purchasing Division to more of a marketing perspective. Win Golden was told to "dress the business up, sell it, shut it down or run it." This industrial protein venture had good growth potential, although not exceptional, and with a better understanding of the market and positioning of its product, it soon became profitable.

FOOD PROTEIN

A second venture developed out of this inherited protein plant. This was called Food Protein and involved developing soy-protein food ingredients. In contrast to Industrial Protein, Food Protein was seen as business with high growth potential. However, it was R & D intensive and aimed at a market which had not yet developed and thus regarded as a longer-term, more speculative venture.

In August 1968, John McCammon, who had worked with Win Golden in the Purchasing department, was transferred to the NVD and made General Manager, Protein department, responsible for both the Industrial Protein and Food Protein ventures. Under him, the Industrial Protein venture's sales and earnings remained steady at approximately

$4 million and $250,000 for the next two years. Food Protein's sales increased from approximately $500,000 in 1968 to $1,000,000 in 1970. Food protein losses for those three years averaged approximately $200,000 per year.

AIRLINE FOOD SERVICES

A third venture was initiated in 1969 - Airline Food Services. It was an attempt to redesign the Wellston, Ohio poultry processing plant to produce high quality frozen dinner for the airline trade. In January 1968, Dr. Guido Girolami was hired as assistant to the Director-NVD Management and was made responsible for developing this venture. In its first year of operation (1969), it nearly broke even on sales of $500,000. It was expected to grow into a profitable operation although there was limited growth potential unless expanded outside of the airline industry.

DAIRY FOOD SYSTEMS

The fourth venture initiated during the first two years of the NVD's operation was called Dairy Food Systems. It was begun almost immediately after the NVD was set up. The business idea was to back-integrate - to produce a milk protein product which the Chow division had been buying from outside suppliers, repackaging and selling at a rate of 11,000 tons per year. This idea had been "floating around the company" for sometime and Win Golden had earlier been involved in investigating it.

An abandoned dairy facility was leased and the NVD began to manufacture this product from whey, a cheese by-product which was considered waste. Given a captive market, known technology, an inexpensive raw material, and a small asset base (a leased plant), this venture was immediately very profitable. It was rapidly expanded by leasing two other facilities, then building a plant. Sales of this venture increased from less than $500,000 in 1968 to $7,000,000 in 1971, and return on assets increased to over 60% in 1971. Through this period a small sales base outside of the company was gradually built, up, but more than 80% of sales were to the Chow Division.

RESEARCH AND DEVELOPMENT

During the 1967-1970 period, Win Golden used a variety of researchers to support the NVD's evaluation and testing of new venture ideas. He had developed a network of contacts in the research organization when he had reviewed corporate R & D policy for top management and he used this network to locate and tap the required technical expertise.

When the NVD was created, an existing protein research group (which had supported the industrial and food protein operations) was transferred from the Purchasing division to the NVD. This group which was initially small in size (with only six researchers) reported directly to Win Golden. It carried out a dual function during the early years of the NVD. It supported the three protein ventures (Diary Food Systems, Industrial Protein and Food Protein) and also provided assistance where required in the evaluation and testing of new venture ideas.

SUMMARY: 1967-1970

During this early period, the NVD maintained a low profile. The two developing "cash cows" - Dairy Food Systems and Industrial Protein - financed the longer-range developmemt expenditures on Food Protein while Airline Foods appeared to be heading into the black.

In 1969, an important conference was held in which a consultant and Ralston Purina's top management evaluated the company's portfolio of businesses considering their long-term growth prospects. They emerged from this conference with the recognition that to meet corporate growth objectives of 10-15% per year, their portfolio of businesses would have to be modified. The company began to withdraw from the poultry processing business later that year and there was an increased importance placed on new ventures both in the operating divisions and in the New Venture Division.

Nevertheless, in 1970, due to its size, funding, low profile, and lack of glamorous ventures, the NVD was still perceived by some to be an activity of little significance and with little likely impact on the corporation.

1970-1972

In the period 1970-1972, the NVD continued to grow and become more profitable. Its combined sales reached approximately $17 million in 1972, with pretax earnings of over $2 million. Return on assets had increased each year from 1967 and in 1972 reached 28%.

PRESSURES TO SPIN-OFF VENTURES

During this period, pressures to have profitable ventures spun-off to the operating division developed. A conflict with the Chow Division centered around the Diary Food Systems venture. It began in about 1970 with a questioning of transfer prices. There was "hall talk" and needling that the New Venture people were getting an excessively high price. Underlying this was the view of the Chow division that the Dairy Food System profits were rightfully theirs, that the majority of production was being sold to them, and thus the venture should be part of the Chow Divison rather than the NVD. There was the expectation that once ventures were operating profitably they would be spun-off. This had been inferred in the NVD's charter and seemed to underlie the whole concept of the department's function.

On the other hand, individuals in the NVD saw the dispute with the Chow Division as "a power play by a large division trying to get hold of a profitable operation." They had several reasons for wanting to retain the venture. Dairy Food System was the NVD's main "cash cow." Its profits were needed to finance other long-term development activities such as Food Protein. Secondly, much of the profits realized in 1971 had been due to selected forward buying of raw materials. It was felt that these should not be passed along to the Chow Division. A third reason was that the NVD felt that they were in a better position to guide the business and that the Chow Division was not marketing the product aggressively enough. A final factor was referred to by Hal Dean:

> Emotionally and politically they naturally want to hang on to ventures.

This dispute went on for several years with the problem resurfacing periodically. Several arbiters were appointed to resolve the issue of the appropriate transfer price at various times but their solutions were only temporary.

Top management stood firmly behind the NVD in permitting it to retain the venture. Hal Dean explained:

> The NVD came out pretty well on this, both on the transfer price and in keeping the venture. A lot of what they were fighting over was raw material profit. This was a "plum" and the issue was how do you divide it up. In a situation like that, you usually try to help the baby. It was more important for the NVD and they deserved it as well.

Win Golden felt that the recommendation in the NVD charter that it determine the timing of the venture spin-off was of importance in giving the NVD a strong position in a conflict of this type.

Meanwhile, the conflict over transfer price "threatened the product's market franchise." It was feared that market share would decline as the Chow Division set prices to take their margins on top of those of the NVD.

In mid-1969, the Consumer Products Division sought to have the Airline Food Services venture transferred to their division. They saw a logical fit with their growing grocery frozen food business. The NVD opposed the positioning of the venture in a "large divisional operation." In addition, they wanted initially to limit the venture to the airlines and high quality hotel and resort markets. The issue was decided in favor of Consumer Products. The venture as conceived of by the NVD would have been limited in size while its greatest potential was in the consumer market. The venture was transferred to the Consumer Products Division in October 1969. It was combined with their frozen foods venture and rapidly expanded. Its losses escalated and it was discontinued in July 1972.

Win Golden did not strongly protest the decision to transfer the Airline Food Service venture, although he felt it would have a greater chance for success in the NVD. It was clear that it had greater long-term growth potential in the Consumer Products Division and it was one of the less important ventures for the NVD.

The experience of facing strong pressure to have two promising ventures pulled out of the NVD appeared to influence the thinking of the individuals in the department. In their subsequent ventures, they shied away from areas in which operating divisions could have a strong claim on the businesses they would develop.

STAFFING AND ORGANIZATION

In 1970, two key individuals were added to the NVD. In January, Dennis Zensen was hired as the Assistant to the Director replacing the individual who was heading up the Airline Food Services venture. As with several other key people in the NVD, including Win Golden and Guido Girolami, he was hired at a point when he was preparing to leave the company. He did not see opportunities which were of interest in Ralston Purina. When he was at corporate headquarters for his exit interview, Hal Dean contacted him to discuss a position. in the NVD. They met three times before he was introduced to Win Golden. Although he was concerned by the lack of definition in the position, he took it at Hal Dean's urging. He explained:

> Hal Dean said, "Take the job, and it will all work out. I've picked a lot of young people for undefined jobs and it has worked out for them."

Paul Hatfield was hired later in the year to head up the Industrial and Food Protein ventures. Although he had had a working relationship with Win Golden several years earlier, he was also "recruited by Hal Dean." He was working in the Foodmaker Division after it was acquired as a liaison with the parent company. He had a break with the president of Foodmaker and was fired. Hal Dean saw him as "a good man falling between the cracks" and recommended him to the NVD. Paul Cornelsen, Ralston's Executive Vice President observed: "It has been our experience that the . type of maverick who may run into difficulties in an established division often finds the NVD an attractive environment."

The Protein Research group within the NVD expanded rapidly during its first four years. Its initial staff of six grew to nearly thirty by the end of 1972.

As shown in Figure 6.2, in the end of 1970, the organization structure was not significantly different than initially planned, although a few individuals had left the department and others had been hired.

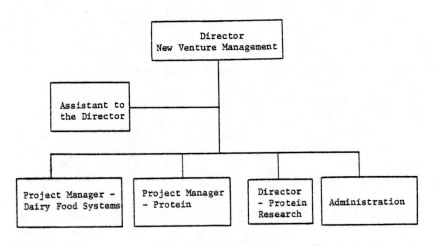

Figure 6-2

MARICULTURE

In 1970, a venture in "mariculture" – growing shrimp in an artifically controlled environment was initiated. Win Golden had become aware of this area through discussions with a researcher in the Chow division, which had been selling feed for fish formulas for catfish and other commercial fish farms.   This researcher was developing custom formulas for different types of fish and believed that this represented an excellent business opportunity.   However, he had been unable to get support for it from the Chow division.   He and Win Golden had several discussions about this and Win began to read up on mariculture.   He soon concluded that the cultivation of shellfish rather than simply providing the feed was a venture idea worth exploring.   When Dennis Zensen joined the department he took on the project and spent about six months studying raising shrimp.

During 1970, the decision was made to go ahead with a three-year research project which would seek to determine the feasibility and economics of shrimp mariculture.   The total budget was less than $1,000,000.

The Mariculture venture was the second "long-shot"-type venture the NVD initiated, the other being Food Protein.   Like Food Protein, it was on the forefront of a new emerging technology.   In 1970, there was no way to assess how long or how much money it would take to develop a commercially viable shrimp mariculture business.   Thus, the strategy adopted was to keep expenditures at a relatively low level so that the NVD could afford to stay with the venture (if warranted) for the "long haul."   The venture was initially classifed as a "research venture" within the NVD.   In 1973, the decision was made to continue it as such and expenditures were increased but still remained modest in relation to the NVD's other activities.   Hal Dean commented on the significance of terming it a "research venture":

> We think of research money differently than money committed to a venture. Research money is an expense - there is no expectation of a viable profitable product. You're buying knowledge. Money spent on a venture is an investment and there is an expectation of a profit. Calling mariculture a "research venture" clears up our thinking about it and creates the proper expectations.

The decision to initiate the Mariculture venture reflected a belief that the technology could be made viable and that with its experience in feed formulas, Ralston Purina was in an excellent position to pioneer in this area.   There was another factor which may have influenced the decision to enter mariculture - it was a new, glamorous industry.   The NVD at that point had succeeded in being profitable, but its ventures with the exeption of food protein did not represent entries into glamorous new businesses.   Mariculture fit the expectations for a venture group - an innovative, exciting business at the forefront of technology.

MUSHROOMS

In 1971, another innovative venture was begun with the objective of growing high quality fresh mushrooms in plants located in the target market. The idea for the venture originated when Hal Dean was contacted by an investment banker representing a mushroom grower who needed capital for expansion of his cannery. The letter which Hal Dean received was passed to Win Golden who assigned Dennis Zensen to investigate. He found the canned mushroom industry of little interest, but was excited by the technology that the grower was considering. Rather than growing his mushrooms in caves and basements as was traditional, this grower planned to build an above-ground climate controlled plant. This would give him a greater proportion of higher quality mushrooms which he airfreighted to the south and sold at a higher profit than he made on his canned mushrooms. The NVD developed the idea of moving the plant to the market and growing mainly for the high margin fresh mushroom market and selling to a cannery only those mushrooms that were of poorer quality. This became the business idea of the venture. It was initiated as a start-up venture and was expanded in 1972 through the acquisition of a mushroom grower and in 1974 through a joint venture with a European mushroom spawn (seed) producer.

SUMMARY

During the first five years of the NVD's existence (1967-1972), its survival was attributed to the fact that it was considered small and relatively insignificant, it was not a major cash drain (and thus it could be of little harm) and it was strongly supported by the Chairman, Hal Dean.

In the summer of 1972, perceptions of the NVD changed.

1972-1974

In Ralston Purina, each August a Budget Committee composed of division General Managers, the Corporate Controller, the Executive Vice President, the Chairman and the President, reviewed the capital requests and operating budgets of each of the divisions.

DEMAND FOR CAPITAL

At the August 1972 Budget Committee meeting, the NVD presented a three-year program for the Food Protein venture. Six months earlier, they had received approval for a first phase expenditure of $7 million on a Food Protein plant in Memphis, Tennessee. This would be the first "scaled up" edible protein facility. Prior to that Food Protein had been operating out of a pilot plant at the Industrial Protein facility.

The three-year plan presented in August requested an immediate second phase expenditure of $16 million on Memphis and total capital expenditures on Food Protein of over $60 million during the next three years. In essence, the Budget Committee faced a "go/no go" decision on expanding a Food Protein venture which had yet to prove itself. The scaled up plant in Memphis was experiencing start-up problems. The venture had had only one marginally profitable year in its five-year history and was in the red in 1972, the market was only beginning to develop, and it was too early to tell how large it would be. The NVD's past record on Food Protein had been that forecasts were based on "ideal" conditions and for several years in a row "abnormal" economic events had occurred and resulted in profits well below those budgeted for. The nature of the business seemed nebulous and foreign to most of the Budget Committee and they were particularly distrubed by its capital intensity. In the proposed Memphis plant, more than four times the investment was required to produce $1.00 of sales as compared to the Chow Division. In addition, substantial investment had to be made in a technical service marketing organization to sell to the venture's industrial accounts. In a company which had built a franchise with the farmer and grocery consumer, the value of an industrial franchise was questioned.

The Budget Committee was not inclined to approve capital expenditures of this magnitude of "untested ground." However, during the summer there were five meetings of the Budget Committee. Hal Dean strongly backed the NVD. The General Manager of one of the operating divisions explained: "What it boiled down to was that Hal felt good about protein and no one could argue with him on the basis of the fundamentals because we were dealing with the unknown." The NVD's request for funds for the Memphis plant was approved.

There is little doubt that Hal Dean was the deciding factor in the decision to expand the Food Protein venture. It was observed that Win Golden and Hal Dean were the only two members of the Budget Committee who enthusiastically promoted the growth plan for Food Protein. The balance of the committee initially favored a more cautious approach." Hal Dean commented:

> A great strength of our management style is that we have strong individuals who are willing to argue hard for their opinions. These decisions were not simply and clearcut and there were sound arguments on both sides. The key is that once the decision was made, they all pulled together like a team.

PROTEIN R&D

Hal Dean's support for the Food Protein venture was reflected in another action taken in 1972. Within the NVD, it was believed that an expanded effort in basic protein research was required in support of Food Protein. However, Win Golden felt that the cost of this effort was more than the NVD could absorb. Thus, he with two key R & D directors laid out ground rules for a corporate program in protein research. This proposal was supported by the head of Corporate R & D and Hal Dean. "With top management support" this program was initiated and given a budget of approxmiately $500,000 per year.

ATTITUDES TOWARD THE END

The debate over the expansion of the Food Protein venture significantly altered how the NVD was viewed within the company. It was no longer an insignificant irritant. If successful, the Food Protein venture could have an important impact - perhaps being the company's "pet food" of the 1980's. More immediately, the NVD began to be seen as a "capital gobbler." One Budget Committee member observed: "With that approval they moved into the big leagues."

The recognition that capital could be allocated to untested NVD ventures over projects in the operating division affected attitudes toward the NVD. There was a growing concern and questioning of the NVD's apparent policy of retaining ventures after they had been operating for several years and/or had become pofitable. As the glamour and profile of the NVD rose and the focus shifted from the early "cash cows" to the newer more speculative ventures, doubts were raised. One individual who was in an operating division at the time commented: "At the end of 1972, Mariculture was seen as a drain on the pocketbook, Mushrooms was a gleam in the eye and Food Protein was running into snags."

CONFLICT WITH OTHER DEPARTMENTS

During 1973, Win Golden recognized that "the divisions were beginning to put us in a plastic bag." The cooperation of the operating divisions and staff departments which they relied on heavily was disappearing. Their people were not as available as they had been earlier, and objection to the NVD's special treatment was growing. A divisional General Manager explained the impact of this:

> Operating division or a staff department can make it more difficult for the NVD to drain the brains of their people. To generate venture ideas you need that. The operating division people can

screen what they talk about or simply shut the door. Ideas don't develop in a vacuum and simply by not helping it, the divisions can hurt the NVD.

At that time, the Food Protein venture was planning a strong effort overseas and growing rapidly. In doing this, it would be invading the very strong, clearly definded historical domain of the International Division which handled overseas sales of all the company's products. It was becoming apparent that some action had to be taken to avoid a squabble with the International Division."

Other lesser conflicts had been developing with staff departments over the special treatment of the NVD. An individual in the legal department explained:

> Being men of action, they would be off doing something without checking with anyone - like registering a trademark or agreeing on contracts which we could not condone. They would say, "leave us alone, when we get bigger we'll bother." It was tough getting them to realize that they were part of a large company, no matter what they called themselves.

Tensions in the NVD's relationship with the Corporate Engineering Department also developed at this time. The usual procedure for designing plants was for Engineering to meet process specifications provided by the operating divisions. When the Memphis plant for the Food Protein venture was to be designed, the NVD hired three engineers without following established procedures. They designed the plant, estimated the cost and wanted to use Corporate Engineering only to oversee the actual construction. The rationale for this was that the plant was fundamentally different than others in the company. It involved a closed continuous process much like a chemical plant and the knowledge and experience of Corporate Engineering was in material handling, mixing and packaging. Nevertheless, by-passing Corporate Engineering and going outside for engineers created resentment which lasted about three years.

In addition, there was a growing competition between the Protein Research groups in the NVD and Corporate Research, however this "friction" never became serious.

REORGANIZATION

In July 1973, steps were taken to alleviate the tensions and conflicts which were developing between the NVD and other departments. Reporting relationships were changed so that the NVD reported to Paul Cornelson, the Executive Vice President who headed the International Division. The protein ventures were given global authority and the protective wing which Hal Dean held over the NVD was partially lifted. In fact, during the next six months Hal Dean incresed his demands on the NVD and often prodded them openly in group meetings. These actions were quite successful in freeing the NVD from the "fair-haired boys" image it had been branded with. In fact, this change in reporting relationships was interpreted by some individuals in the NVD and elsewhere in the company as moving the NVD "down a notch."

IMPROVED RELATIONS

The NVD's relationships with other departments in the company improved during 1973. However, Hal Dean's more critical approach to the department was again raising questions about its worth and the view that it had been a cash drain was becoming accepted among top management and the Board of Directors. At a meeting of the Board in early 1975, Hal Dean was particularly critical of the NVD. Win Golden responded to this by preparing a review of the NVD's total expenses, P&L, and return on assets from 1967-1974. It showed a return on assets of over 10%.[2] He presented this to Hal Dean and it was reviewed with the Board of Directors at the next meeting. This report and its presentation to the Board were key actions intended to rebuild support for the NVD and re-establish its credibility.

SUMMARY: 1972-1974

The period 1972-1974 was a difficult transition for the NVD. It was given strong support by Hal Dean as it rose from insignificance to a "capital gobbling" division. It then met with resistance from other sub-units of the corporation but this was countered by transferring it away from the "protective wing" of the Chairman and giving it more even-handed treatment. When Win Golden felt that the pendulum was swinging too far against him, he made a strong argument on behalf of the NVD. His political acumen and Hal Dean's support and sensitivity to the changing views and attitudes in the company were critical factors. In reference to the former, one individual observed:

> Win Golden did a great job of walking the tight rope between the divisions and the staff departments. It takes fancy footwork to get into someone's bailiwick and not have them fight.

1974-1976

In early 1974, the NVD was riding on a wave of expansion. The Diary Food and Industrial Protein ventures were continuing to grow and remain profitable with their sales increasing by almost 50% from 1973 to 1974. Food Protein sales tripled in 1974 and the venture earned close to $2 million. One member of the department described the feeling in the NVD in early 1974:

> We felt we were on the edge of breaking away. We had earned our stripes and were preparing to prove the cynics wrong. We thought we stood on good ground.

CORPORATE CONSOLIDATION

By mid-1974, the outlook for the economy had become uncertain and there were "dark clouds on the horizon." Top management decided to cut back across the whole corporation - both reducing planned capital expenditures and tightening up on expense budgets. In August 1974, the NVD proposed a three-year capital budget to $150 million. That began what was described as "a long, hot summer."

The total capital spending plans of the divisions for the year 1975 substantially exceeded the amount top management wanted to spend. The result was a series of Budget Committee meetings in which each division's projects were reviewed and it was decided which would be funded.

There were strong pressures to defer the projects proposed by the NVD. Several cost reduction projects from operating divisions with returns on investment as high as 50% and minimal risk had been proposed and were deferred. In the Budget Committee sessions during the summer of 1974, Hal Dean took a more tempered approach than he had in 1972 in support of the NVD. The NVD's three-year capital request of $150 million was finally cut by two-thirds to a "franchise maintenance program" of $48 million. As part of the trimming, a $25 million Food Protein plant to be built in Pryor, Oklahoma was delayed by the committee. However, top management's continued support of the NVD was reflected eight months later when it was decided that capital spending could by increased. The Pryor, Oklahoma plant was the first deferred project to be reinstated. In reflecting on this period, Hal Dean commented:

> We were looking ahead to a recession and we cut everbody back. But losing the Pryor plant was a great trauma in the NVD. They

wanted to go ahead full blast. Making them slow down was a good lesson and as a result, they did a better job.

The magnitude of the NVD capital request of $150 million in the face of a "capital crunch" further opened eyes within the company to the proportions that its activities were reaching. It also served to reinforce the realization that capital was allocated to the NVD at some expense to the other divisions.

VENTURE GENERATION

The corporate consolidation in 1974 also affected the venture generating activities of the NVD. Up to that point, these had been irregular.

Prior to 1970, the department's energies were focused on the on-going ventures which had been inherited or come about through trouble-shooting, rather than being initiated through a formal search activity.

From 1970 to 1972, there were periodic brain-storming sessions among Win Golden, his assistant, and the two project managers. In time, a methodology of generating and evaluating ideas was developed and seemed to be promising. However, the demands of operations forced them to give up this activity. During this time, outside consultants were hired to "screen" sectors of the economy for promising ideas but these were not fruitful.

In mid-1972, Win Golden hired an individual to carry out the search for venture ideas and this function was temporarily revitalized. However, the Mushroom venture soon began to take up this individual's full time and for about six months there were no venture generation activity. The Mushroom venture was then handed over to another individual and venture generation started up again.

In August 1974, the budget for venture generation activities was eliminated for the first time. The primary rationale was not to cut expenses but rather that ventures generated would create additional future capital demands.

The sporadic formal venture generating efforts were designed to screen and capture ideas of merit. All ventures initiated by the NVD were either ideas inherited with its formation, ideas which had been floating around the company, or ideas brought to an NVD member's attention. Nevertheless, it was felt that the formal screening function was effective in identifying viable ideas.

DIFFICULTIES IN MUSHROOM VENTURE

Toward the end of 1974, the Mushroom venture began to run into difficulty. Prior to that, there had been a growing feeling of confidence and expectations for it.

It had been decided that the initial plant would be located in Florida to serve that state and parts of Georgia. The market was tested by flying in fresh mushrooms for the north, selling them through a supermarket chain, and tracking individual consumers. The results of these early market tests were extremely positive. The rate of consumption of mushrooms for individual consumers increased about ten-fold. Thus, in additon to replacing canned mushrooms, it was believed that the venture could expect a tremendous increase in primary demand for mushrooms.

The viability of the production system then became the key unknown. The only way to test it was to build a plant. Win Golden observed:

> We have always tried to test our ventures on as small a scale as possible, but mushrooms was one venture which defied a mini-test.

The plant in Zellwood, Florida was designed to have a highly automated harvesting system to replace the traditional labor intense handpicking. In late 1974, it became apparent that the automated harvesting system in the Zellwood plant would not work. A few months later, the NVD proposed scrapping $1.5 million of equipment in the Zellwood plant and redesigning it to use manual harvesting. They simultaneously proposed expanding the business into another market with a second plant! Again, the NVD was in the position of facing a reluctant Budget Committee. They did not want to commit to a second plant before the first was operating satisfactorily. The NVD argued that once the business idea was proven, which they felt it had been, they had to expand rapidly in the face of new competitors attracted to the industry. The funds for both plants were obtained.

HAL DEAN'S SUPPORT

As had occurred several times in the past, the NVD proposed an aggressive, rapid expansion program for an unproven venture and Hal Dean was an important factor in obtaining Budget Committee approval.

Through the NVD's nine-year history, Hal Dean's support was reflected in several ways. In Budget Committee meetings he often argued "objectively but forcefully" for funding of NVD projects. Because of his management style and the organizational positioning of the NVD he had become involved in ventures early in the idea development stage. Thus, he influenced and shaped projects as in their early conception. When these were brought to the Budget Committee, he could take an advocacy position because his objections had largely been rectified before they reached the Budget Committee.

His sensitivity to the attitudes and feelings within the company was commented on by several individuals. When controversies appeared to be developing, he moved quickly and directly to resolve them before they could grow. He felt that communication was the key to getting support for the NVD among lower-level people in the other departments. He explained: "I myself had to explain what we were trying to do and why, to as many people in the company as possible."

Ralston Purina had established a Management Advisory Board and a Corporate Development Board made up of middle-level mangers. Hal Dean met with both groups and discussed corporate objectives and the NVD and he felt that this had been important in building lower-level support.

In managing the NVD, he felt it was necessary to carefully balance support and demands. At each step of the way he combined these to meet the situation. Initially in 1967, he gave support in the form of a "dowry" and a direct reporting relationship while he also put the demand to "pay your own way." Later he supported the NVD in its capital requests but also lifted his "proctective wing" and shifted the NVD to Paul Cornelsen. In meetings, he sometimes strongy supported the NVD but at other times he led the attack on it - his favorite saying being: "so far, all you've given me is promises." This careful balancing of support and demands was seen as an important factor in allowing the NVD to overcome various hurdles as it developed.

MATURATION INTO AN OPERATING GROUP

During 1974 and 1975, it became quite clear that the NVD was evolving into an operating division. Venture generation search and screening activities had been discontinued in late 1974 and all of the ventures except for Mariculture were producing products which were sold commercially.

In about mid-1975, Win Golden, Paul Cornelson, and Hal Dean began to discuss the future role of the NVD. Win Golden wanted it to be designated as the company's fifth "group," the others being the Agricultural Products Group, the Consumer Products Group, the Restaurant Group, and the Intenational Group. In October 1975, this change was made. The department's ventures--Agribioculture (Mushrooms), Protein (incorporating both Industrial Protein and Food

Protein), Dairy Food Systems, and the research venture in Mariculture--
were designed as divisions within the "New Venture Management"
Group.

These four divisions were run by two Vice Presidents - Dennis
Zensen and Paul Hatfield.   The former was responsible for
Agribioculture and Mariculture while the two protein based ventures
(Dairy Food Systems and Protein) reported to the latter.   These two
individuals were given broad operation control within their businesses.

The organizational change of October 1975 was formal
recognition that the NVD had matured.   However, rather than
abandoning its venture generating activites, these were revitalized.   In
June 1976, an individual was hired to reinitiate venture search and
screening activities and the New Venture Group took on the dual
responsibility of managing its operating division and identifying and
developing new business opportunities.

SITUATION IN 1976

In 1976, Ralston Purina was in an enviable position. Company
sales and earnings reached record levels with return on equity over 15%.
Despite fluctuations in commodity prices, earnings had increased eight of
the previous nine years.

The troublesome transitional period of the late sixties was a thing
of the past. In fact, in 1976, Ralston Purina was included in Dun's
Review's list of five best managed American companies.

The New Venture Group was also continuing its growth in sales
and contribution.   The department had gained acceptance within the
company although there was some question as to whether the new dual
role (launching new ventures and managing on-going ones) would be a
viable one. Win Golden believed that his Group could effectively carry
out this dual mission because the high degree of autonomy given Dennis
Zensen and Paul Hatfield freed him to concentrate on new ventures. He
foresaw the group organized as shown in Figure 6-3.

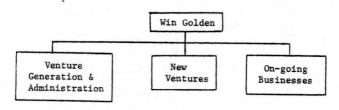

Figure 6-3

NOTES

[1]Although in 1967 there was uncertainty as to the future growth of the pet food business, it has continued to be a rapid growth area through the mid-1970's.

[2]This excludes a relatively small corporate expense budget which covers venture search activities and overhead unrelated to individual ventures.

CHAPTER 7

PHASE II: FINDINGS AND INTERPRETATION OF CASES

Chapter 7 will be presented in two parts. In Part I, I will discuss the factors which influence the *direction* of NVD evolution drawing on illustrative examples from the three indepth cases as well as several of the fifteen other NVDs studied in less depth. I will conclude the first part of this chapter with a framework that explains (and allows one to predict) the direction of NVD evolution.

In part II, I will review and analyze each of the three case studies presented in the preceding chapters. The discussion will focus on the situational factors which appear to have influenced their *path* of evolution. I will conclude the second part of the chapter with a discussion of an apparent relationship between the mission of the NVD and the pressures for maturation, redefinition and elimination.

Direction vs. Path of NVD Evolution

The distinction between the *direction* of an NVD's evolution and the specific *path* it follows is central to both the organization of this chapter and the broader argument presented in this thesis.

Direction

As explained in Chapter 3, NVD's were found to evolve in one of two directions - "emergence" or "decline." When an NVD was "emerging," its size, importance and impact on the parent company were growing. When an NVD was "declining," its size, importance and impact on the parent company were decreasing.

Two clusters of factors were found to be the main influences on the NVD's direction and evolution. I have called these the "corporate strategic posture" and the "NVD political posture." These will be discussed in Part I.

Path

Five specific paths along which NVDs evolve were identified. As shown in Figure 7-1, two of these were in the direction of emergence while three were in the direction of decline:

DIRECTION	• EMERGENCE	• DECLINE
	• Evolution Toward MACRO NVD	• Evolution Toward MICRO NVD
Path	• Maturation	• Redefinition
		• Elimination

Figure 7-1. NVD Evolution

Although the two clusters of factors mentioned above (the "corporate strategic posture" and the "NVD political posture") appear to have determined the direction of evolution in the cases studied, the specific paths followed were determined by a variety of "situational" factors. That is, they were specific to each case and could not be generalized across companies. The factors influencing the path of NVD evolution will be discussed in the second part of this chapter.

The purpose of this chapter is to provide an understanding of how the roles and functions of an NVD evolve over time. This is of more than just academic interest. It will be argued in Chapter 8 that understanding how and why NVDs evolve will allow managers to plan for this process, influence it and perhaps control it as desired.

PART I: FACTORS DETERMINING THE DIRECTION OF NVD EVOLUTION

Two clusters of factors - the "corporate strategic posture" and the "NVD political posture" - appeared to determine the direction of an NVD's evolution. These are discussed in the two sections which follow.

CORPORATE STRATEGIC POSTURE

Overview

The "corporate strategic posture" refers to the cycles of diversification and consolidation that typically characterize corporate growth. A corporation's "strategic posture" at any given point in time can be positioned on a continuum, one end of which is a "diversifying" posture, while the other end is a "consolidating" posture.

Four factors appear to determine a corporation's positioning on this continuum. The first is the company's corporate strategy at the time. Does the corporate strategy emphasize diversification, expansion of sales in new areas, and new business development or does it emphasize cost reduction, improving efficiency and margins, and/or the support of the company's existing businesses? The second factor is the company's financial position. Does it have excess funds, is slack being generated, are the balance sheet ratios improving, or is it in a tight cash position with capital rationing and perhaps a balance sheet which is weakening? The third factor is the situation of the primary industry that the company is in. Does it appear to be contracting in size, becoming unprofitable, or maturing, suggesting that the company should look elsewhere for future business opportunities or does it have a favorable outlook with attractive opportunities on the horizon? The final factor influencing the corporate strategic posture is the orientation of top management. Is top management enterpreneurial and risk taking or is it conservative and risk averse?

The main influences on the corporate strategic posture are summarized in Figure 7-2.

Factor	Diversifying	Consolidating
CORPORATE STRATEGY	• Diversification and expansion into new areas • Emphasis on increasing sales	• Consolidation • Emphasis on cost reduction, improving efficiency and margins and support of existing operations
FINANCIAL POSITION	• Excess funds • Slack generated • Balance sheet improving	• Tight cash • Capital rationing • Balance sheet weakening
INDUSTRY SITUATION	• Unfavorable • Outlook	• Favorable outlook
TOP MANAGEMENT ORIENTATION	• Entrepreneurial • Risk taking	• Conservative • Risk averse

Figure 7-2. Corporate Strategic Posture

To the extent that a corporation is in a diversifying posture, there appear to be pressures for the NVD to emerge. If it is a MICRO

NVD, it will tend to evolve toward becoming a MACRO NVD. There will also be a tendency for it to retain ventures longer and mature into an operating division.

To the extent that a corporation is in a consolidating posture, there are pressures for the NVD to decline. If it is a MACRO NVD, it will tend to evolve into a MICRO NVD. There will also be heightened pressures for redefinition and elimination.

Prior Research

The contention that the "corporate strategic posture" is a major influence on an NVD's evolution is supported by the earlier research of others in the fields of Business Policy and Organizational Behavior.

Learned, Christensen, Andrews and their associates at the Harvard Business School[1] have argued that organization structure should be used to implement corporate strategy. Their normative theory is that sub-unit missions and objectives should reflect an overall corporate strategy and as the strategy changes, sub-unit missions should evolve accordingly. The view that corporate strategy is a driving force for the evolution of an NVD's mission is thus consistent with their prescriptions for how corporations should be managed.

The impact of the corporate financial position - specifically, the availability of "slack" resources - on NVD evolution is supported by research at Carnegie-Mellon University by Richard Cyert, James March, and Herbert Simon.

March and Simon wrote in 1958 that "slack money or manpower" may stimulate formation of an "investing" or "entrepreneurial function."[2] A decade later, Cyert and March[3] argued that innovative activity such as research and development (or new ventures) were often a major use of "slack" or excess resources within a firm. Thus, in their view, changes in a company's financial position would clearly be expected to impact on the role of an NVD.

The influence of an unfavorable industry outlook on NVD evolution also appears to be consistent with the research conducted at Carnegie. March and Simon have written that organizations are induced to change their "program of activity" when a change in the environment makes existing activities unsatisfactory. Specifically:

"We would predict efforts t oward innovation in a company whose. . .total profits or rate of return on investment had declined."[4]

Extending their argument further, it seems logical that an unfavorable industry outlook - creating the *expectations* of declining profits - would similarly impact on innovative activities - in this case on NVD's mission.

Finally, the research of Zeleznick strongly supports the contention that top management orientation is a critical determinant of an NVD's evolution. In *Human Dilemmas of Leadership*, he has linked the personality orientation of leaders to their organization's tendency to defend the status quo or actively seek out new opportunities.[5] Thus, one would expect that a change in top management personnel could influence an NVD's role and mission and perhaps even bring about its elimination.

To summarize, past research as well as the empirical data discussed below appear to support the contention that the "corporate strategic posture" is a critical influence on NVD evolution.

Analysis

The three case studies presented earlier plus interviews at other companies with NVDs have indicated that one or more of the four factors above (top management orientation, industry situation, financial position, and corporate strategy) were the primary driving forces leading to the establishment of the NVD.

ENTREPRENEURIAL TOP MANAGEMENT

In many companies which had established NVDs, there was an individual in top management who was singled out as "entrepreneurial."

At Standard Chemical, Ken Anderson was clearly more "entrepreneurial" than the presidents who had preceded him. He was described as "dynamic and aggressive", "a very strong president who had vision, was articulate and strong-willed." Before becoming president, he had headed up the fastest growing segment of the company's business, the International Division and in that position he had pushed for rapid expansion abroad.

During his tenure as President, Ken Anderson was the strongest proponent of diversification among top management at Standard Chemical. In fact, looking back on the rise and fall of the NVD, one former NVD General Manager commented that "the President simply outran the Executive Committee."

Hal Dean, at Ralston Purina was similarly an "entrepreneurial" chief executive--perhaps even more so than Ken Anderson. He was described by various members of management as "entrepreneurial," "ambitious" and "growth oriented." During the late sixties, Ralston's acquisition and new venture activities reported to him and he was actively and directly involved in the search for and implementation of diversification opportunities.

At DuPont Company, the influence of an entrepreneurial orientation in top management was less clear. Top management shared an orientation toward growth through internal development of new products, but there was no single individual who stood out as an entrepreneur or spokesman for entrepreneurship. The initiation of the Development Department's venture program did not coincide with a change in top management, nor did its decline.

At several of the fifteen other companies in which interviews were conducted, there was an entrepreneurial individual or orientation in top management which appeared to be a driving force behind the establishment of the NVD. At Electronics Corporation of America (see Appendix 3-1), the chairman strongly valued entrepreneurship and the structure of the NVD reflected this. Venture managers as well as other individuals in the company bought shares in the venture, and the venture manager had the opportunity to become a "millionaire" if his venture was successful. Another example is provided by Diversified Chemical Company (also in Appendix 3-1), where venture management had been the traditional career path in the company and the chairman and president were both former venture managers.

UNFAVORABLE INDUSTRY OUTLOOK

A second driving force for the establishment of an NVD was an unfavorable industry outlook. Quite often, an NVD was set up to diversify out of an industry which appeared to have matured or was declining. It should be emphasized that as with an entrepreneurial top management orientation, this was not a necessary condition for establishing an NVD but rather one which was quite common.

An unfavorable industry outlook (maturing or declining) was clearly a motivation for setting up NVDs at both Standard Chemical and Ralston Purina.

In the case of the former, top management believed that the chemical industry was maturing--that its growth rate was "flattening out." The industry had been invaded by the oil companies during the sixties (pricing their product "like it was a gas war") and it was feared that industry profitability would also decline.

At Ralston Purina, it was similarly believed that the company was too heavily involved in maturing industries. There was little doubt that the feed and poultry businesses were mature, expected to grow at the rate of the economy as a whole. The pet food business which had provided the growth of the sixties still had a favorable short and medium term outlook in 1967 but was expected to level off by the mid-seventies. Thus, in both Standard Chemical and Ralston Purina, the desire to diversify out of an industry with an unfavorable outlook (chemicals; feed and poultry) was a reason for setting up the NVD.

Several other companies provide similar examples of NVDs set up to provide an "escape" from an industry with an unfavorable future. Examples include the following:

1. An oil company which saw its business threatened in the long term by alternate sources of energy and constrained raw materials supplies..

2. Several producers of bulk commodity products that saw little opportunity for improved profit margins or return on capital in their existing businesses.

3. A trading stamp company which saw little opportunity for increased market penetration and threats to the trading stamp concept coming from consumer groups, legislation and new types of retail promotions.

EXCESS FUNDS

A third driving force for the establishment of an NVD was a corporate financial position characterized by a surplus of projected cash flow versus projected investment opportunities. This was often found in combination with an unfavorable industry outlook (as a mature industry is often populated by companies with a surplus cash flow)

Two of the most dramatic examples of a surplus cash flow as a driving force for establishment of an NVD were provided by DuPont and Standard Chemical.

In the case of the former, several individuals pointed to the surplus of funds (in excess of investment opportunities) as the single most important factor in bringing about the company's new venture effort. The surplus and cash flow was also seen by at least one Executive Committee member as the primary driving force for the adoption of a corporate strategy of diversification as well as the MACRO approach of the Development department.

At Standard Chemical, a surplus cash flow was also a key reason for establishing the NVD. This "investment gap" as it was often referred to dominated the plans of the NVD and was an important variable in top management's long range planning.

DIVERSIFICATION STRATEGY

A strategy of diversification is implicit in the establishment of an NVD as the NVD's purpose is to launch "new businesses." However, an NVD may exist in a company whose dominant strategy is not one of diversification particularly if its ventures are closely related to the company's existing businesses and/or the NVD follows a MICRO approach.

A newly adopted strategy of diversification was found to be a driving force for establishing the NVD in most of the companies studied. However, its role as a driving force was usually secondary--that is, it resulted from one or more of the other driving forces discussed above.

In the case of Ralston Purina, the diversification strategy resulted from both Hal Dean's personal orientation (dynamic and aggresive), his ambitions for the company and the belief that its businesses were maturing. At Standard Chemical, the primary factors were excess funds and an unfavorable industry outlook. At DuPont, surplus of funds appeared to be the primary driving force for the diversification strategy and the new venture effort.

The most important primary and secondary driving forces for the establishment of the three NVDs studied in depth are summarized in Figure 7-3.

Driving Force: Changing Corporate Situation

When an NVD is established, it usually represents a "fit" with the corporate situation at that specific point in time. That is, the corporate situation in terms of the four factors discussed above (the corporate financial position, the industry situation, the orientation of top management, and the corporate strategy) has created a perceived need for the NVD. However, all four of these factors are variable. Not only are they subject to change, but they are very rarely stable.

Thus, in time the corporate situation inevitably changes and a "misfit" develops between the function of the NVD and the direction the corporation is moving in. Pressures to rectify this misfit develop and these become driving forces for the NVD's evolution. As shown in Figure 7-4, these driving forces push the NVD either in the direction of "emergence" or "decline."

The "misfits" which became driving forces in the three case studies are discussed in part II of this chapter, however, to illustrate this point two examples are provided below:

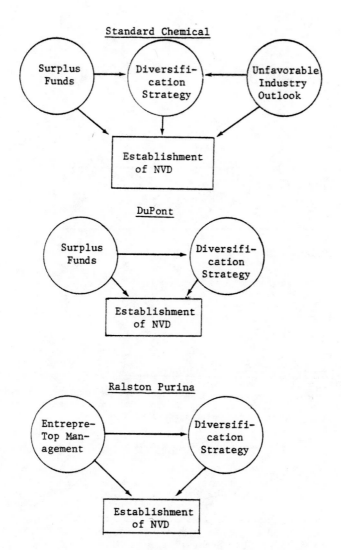

Figure 7-3. Driving Forces for the Establishment of NVDs

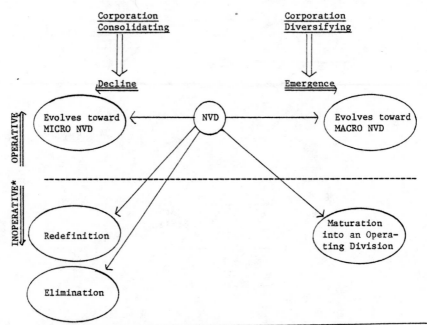

*NVDs which have been Redefined or have Matured are considered "Inoperative" because they no longer have as their <u>main</u> function the commercialization of new ventures. Nevertheless, the department may remain intact with a modified function.

Figure 7-4. Corporate Strategic Situation/NVD Evolution

During the period 1969-1971 at DuPont corporate strategy shifted from one of diversification to consolidation. A misfit was created between the mission of the Development department (to launch large scale ventures) and the modified corporate strategy. Pressures to rectify this misfit became a driving force behind the "decline" of the Development department as an NVD.

In 1970, Ken Anderson, the President of Standard Chemical retired. He was replaced by an individual who was less entrepreneurial--more traditional and conservative. The orientation of top management shifted, creating a misfit between the NVD's mission and top management's ambitions and objectives for the company. Pressures to rectify this misfit became a driving force behind the "decline" of the NVD.

Summary

To summarize the discussion above, it has been argued that the following four factors combine to create a given "corporate strategic posture:"

1.   Industry outlook
2.   Top management orientation
3.   Corporate financial position
4.   Corporate strategy

In response to this corporate strategic posture an NVD is created. In time, the corporate situation changes and the function and mission of the NVD no longer are consistent with it. Pressures to rectify this misfit become a driving force behind the NVD's evolution. When the company is in a "diversifying" posture, pressures are strongest for the NVD to emerge. When the corporation is in a "consolidating" posture, the opposite is the case and there are strong pressures for the NVD to decline.

NVD POLITICAL POSTURE

Overview

The NVD's "political posture" was found to be the other major driving force behind its evolution. The NVD political posture refers to the rising or falling power, credibility, and support for the NVD within the parent corporation. At any point in time, the NVD's "political posture" can be considered either "building" or "eroding" to a varying degree depending on four factors. The first is the sponsorship of the NVD. Does the NVD have a top management sponsor? Is the power of the sponsor within the organization and his support for the NVD rising or falling? The second factor is the relationship of the NVD with other departments and divisions of the company. Is the NVD gaining or losing the support, cooperation, and assistance of other departments and divisions? A third factor is the sub-unit objectives of the NVD. Is the manager of the NVD a strong leader or a weak one? Does he aspire to corporate advancement and is he using the NVD to "build an empie" or is he less aggressive and satisfied with the status quo? A final determinant of the political posture of the NVD is its track record--its perceived performance. What expectations were generated for the NVD?

Has the past performance of the NVD been considered favorable or unfavorable? Has it been regarded as a success or failure?

In Figure 7-5, the main influences on an NVD's political posture are summarized.

Factor	Building	Eroding
SPONSORSHIP OF NVD	• Sponsor and (and) • Increasing power and support of sponsor	• No sponsor (or) • Decreasing power and support of sponsor
RELATIONSHIP WITH OTHER DEPARTMENTS	• Improving • Gaining support and cooperation	• Worsening • Losing support and cooperation
SUB-UNIT OBJECTIVES NVD	• Strong, aggressive and ambitious NVD manager • NVD manager empire building	• Weak, low key, and unambitious NVD manager • NVD manager accepts status quo
PERCEIVED PERFORMANCE OF NVD	• Realistic expectations • Good track record • Considered success	• Excessively high expectations • Poor track record • Considered failure

Figure 7-5. NVD Political Posture

To the extent that an NVD's political posture is "building," it tends to emerge - that is, evolve toward maturation and if it is a MICRO NVD, evolve toward becoming a MACRO NVD. When the NVD political posture is "eroding," the NVD tends to decline.

Prior Research

Earlier in this chapter, it was argued that a corporation's "strategic posture" is a major driving force behind the evolution of its

NVD. In this section, I am suggesting that there is a second major influence - the NVD's "political posture." This contention appears to be consistent with earlier research in Business Policy - most notably, the findings of Joseph Bower in his study of capital investment decisions in a large, diversified chemical company.[6]

Bower's major conclusion - one which challenged the traditional view of resource allocation - was that major investment decisions were the outcome of a multi-level political process rather than being made by a top-level "rational actor." The important variables in Bower's portrayal of the resource allocation process were not return-on-investment or payback, but rather the objectives and ambitions of sub-unit managers, their credibility and track records, and the willingness of general managers to provide "impetus" or sponsorship for projects initited by their subordinates.

In focusing on the NVD's "political posture," I am arguing that much the same variables are critical influences on an NVD's "evolution".

Analysis

The four main factors which appeared to influence the NVD's "political posture" are discussed below.

Sponsorship

Most NVDs were established with the support of a top management "sponsor" (i.e., Hal Dean at Ralston Purina, Ken Anderson at Standard Chemical). As shown in Figure 7-6 a sponsor's long -term support of the NVD appeared to be a function of his commitment, his position in the company, and his leadership style.

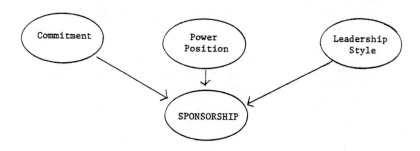

Figure 7-6. Sponsorship of NVD

COMMITMENT

The sponsor's commitment to the NVD can weaken as a result of a variety of factors. He may become impatient and decide that the NVD's activities are not paying off quickly enough or do not warrant the required investment of management time and personnel. Or, he may not want to risk his own position or credibility for the sake of the NVD. The passage of time without a noticeable impact or a decline in corporate earnings may diminish his enthusiam for venturing. The NVD is only one of many concerns and internal "battles." As these other concerns rise and fall in intensity, his support for the NVD is affected.

At Standard Chemical, by the early 1970s, the NVD was well down on the list of issues facing the Executive Committee. At Ralston Purina, Hal Dean's concerns with the transitions underway in corporate control and management style limited the amount of support that he wanted to or was able to give the NVD. This was one of the reasons he instructed Win Golden to keep a low profile when the NVD was set up.

POSITION

The sponsor's position in the company may rise or fall - and there often are corresponding effects felt by the NVD, particularly where the sponsor does not represent the majority view toward the NVD. In several companies, the Board of Directors or division general managers did not support the NVD concept. As a result, when the sponsor of the NVD left the company or "dropped his guard," the NVD was eliminated or redefined.   In one company, the NVD manager stated:

> "The venture division was disbanded, not because of its own performance, either successes or failures, but because of the business downturn which resulted in Board pressure and the President's eventual departure from the company. The new President who replaced him was more traditional and not a supporter of the NVD concept."

At another company, a manager stated that the NVD was disbanded because the Chairman, its chief sponsor, was killed in an accident. At a third company, venture activities were discontinued when the financial vice-president who was their chief sponsor was passed over for the President's position and left the company.

At Standard Chemicals, it was observed that there was a lack of strong commitment for the NVD on the part of the Executive Committee. It rejected most of the minority equity investments and acquisition proposals advanced by the NVD. In 1970, the retirement of the President (the NVD's chief sponsor) opened the door for the NVD's redefinition.

LEADERSHIP STYLE

In addition to the sponsor's committment to the NVD and his position in one company, the third factor which appeared to affect his support for the NVD was his leadership style. By leadership style, I refer to the nature of the relationship between a leader and his peers and subordinates. Leadership style encompasses all aspects of that relationship, but that which appeared to be most relevant to the provision of support for the NVD was:

> "Directive" versus "Democratic" Leadership. Does the sponsor make decisions himself and then "sell" them to his peers and subordinates? Does he try to impose his views of what should be done on others? or Does he present issues to a larger group for them to resolve? Does he attempt to lead through consensus and compromises?

The difference between the two leadership styles which I refer to as "directive" and "democratic" is only a matter of degree, however, it appeared that sponsors with a "directive" leadership style were more willing and better able to support the NVD than those with a "democratic" style.

Ken Anderson of Standard Chemical and Hal Dean of Ralston Purina were two executives who had rather "directive" leadership styles. It was observed that at Standard Chemical, the chief executives who proceeded Ken Anderson were typically "democratic" leaders. In referring to them, one Executive Committee member used the term "judicial leaders." They regularly sought out and followed the counsel of the other members of the Executive Committee. Ken Anderson had a different leadership style, taking a more active role in "leading" the Executive Committee. He often reached a decision and then attempted to "sell" it to the other members of the Committee.

Hal Dean at Ralston-Purina had a similar leadership style, perhaps even more "directive." This was quite clearly demonstrated at the Budget Committee meeting in August, 1972. At that meeting, the NVD had requested $16 million for a protein plant. Hal Dean "felt good about the protein venture" and was in favor of an investment in full scale production facilities. The other Budget Committee members disagreed but were persuaded to follow him.

In both companies--Ralston Purina and Standard Chemical--the chief executive's leadership style appeared to facilitate the provision of support for the NVD.

Relations with Other Divisions

The NVD's relations with other divisions are typically characterized by at least some degree of resentment and lack of cooperation. Resistance to the NVD can be reflected in overt "pot-shots" and active attempts to undermine the department, but more often it is more subtle--a refusal to actively assist the NVD and cooperate with it. This subtle form of resistance became evident at Ralston Purina in 1973 when the division started to "put the NVD in a bag." Their people became less available than they had been earlier, they screened out potentially useful information when talking to the NVD and voluntered little.

At Standard Chemical, the NVD was criticized "behind closed doors." At other companies, resentment of the NVD was similarly reflected in "hall talk" and a subtle lack of cooperation rather than overt actions.

Several factors contributed to this typical reaction of other departments in companies where an NVD was established. Figure 7-7 shows the factors which appeared to be the most significant.

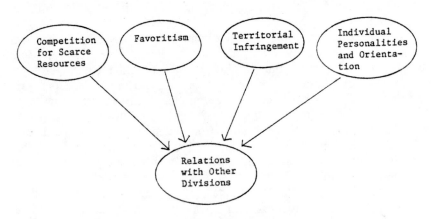

Figure 7-7. Relations with Oher Divisions

COMPETITION FOR SCARCE RESOURCES

First, the NVD represents competition for scarce resources: capital, top management time, and personnel. The scarcer these resources are, the more of a threat the NVD is and the more negative the divisional response.

At Ralston-Purina, the operating division's resistance to the NVD was strongest at two points--when the size of its capital demands became apparent (that the NVD wanted a big slice of the "pie") and when the company cut back on capital expenditures in 1974 (the overall size of the pie shrunk).

At Standard Chemical, the NVD posed a clear threat to the operating divisions in the competition for capital. Its 1971 three year plan set an objective of filling a major part of the $1000 million "gap" in projected sales for 1980. Undoubtably this would require substantial capital. The capital demands of the NVD in its early years represented only the tip of the iceberg. It was anticipated that the NVD's demand for capital to expand the successful ventures in the late seventies would be far greater. The three year plan stated:

> "The NVDs program should place major emphasis on the following. . .making small but hopefully significant beginning steps in NVD type venture businesses so that when capital is available, the growth opportunities of the late seventies are ready."

Thus, the operating divisions "did not welcome" the NVD and withheld their support.

The recruitment of personnel from the operating divisions was another source of irritation in relations between the NVD and operating divisions. In both Standard Chemical and Ralston-Purina, the chairman in the company helped to recruit for the NVD and provided access to personnel in the operating divisions. However, this practice did not endear the NVD to the divisions that were "raided" for personnel.

FAVORITISM

A second source of conflict was the "favoritism" shown toward the NVD. This was reflected in statements made by top management. actions taken on behalf of the NVD, its placement in the organization, and its exemption from standard operating procedures.

In both Standard Chemical and Ralston Purina, the NVD was viewed as "the fair-haired boys." At Standard Chemical, the chairman's continued reference to the NVD as the "brightest" people in the company appeared to create resentment and jealousy. At Ralston-Purina, Hal Dean's active support of the NVD and the favoritism he showed at budget committee meetings produced the same negative reaction. The fact that organizationally the NVD was on the same level as a much larger operating division and reported to the chief executive or Executive Committee also appeared to create resentment at both companies.

The NVD's exemption from standard operating procedures and its tendency to try to avoid corporate legal and accounting "red tape" created conflict with staff departments.   At Ralston-Purina, venture managers signed contracts with customers and registered trademarks without following the procedures set by the Legal department.   An individual in that department complained that "it was tough getting them to realize that they were part of a large company, no matter what they called themselves."   At both Standard Chemical and Ralston-Purina, the corporate engineering department did not have the requisite skills and engineers were hired directly by the NVD rather than through the corporate engineering department.   At both companies, this resulted in a drawn out battle.

TERRITORIAL INFRINGEMENT

A third factor influencing the NVD's relations with other operating departments was its mission.   When it infringed on an operating division's territory by pursuing a venture closely related to that division's business, conflicts often developed around the marketing organizations, positioning the products and transfer pricing.   Conflicts also sometimes developed over the timing of the spin-off of related ventures, with operating divisions wanting to pull the ventures out of the NVD as soon as possible--if a promising venture, often even before it became profitable.

The Dairy Foods venture at Ralston Purina provides an excellent example of this.   As was described in the case study, the Dairy Foods venture represented back-integration for Ralston Purina.   The NVD began production of a product which was repackaged and sold by the Chow division.   For the first few years, more than three-fourths of the venture's sales were to the Chow division.   When it became apparent that the venture was extremely profitable (with a return on investment of over 40%), the Chow division sought to take over the venture or have the transfer price lowered.

These conflicts sometimes pushed the NVD toward ventures which were farther afield and could not be claimed by an existing operating division.   At Ralston Purina, the experience of facing strong pressure to have two ventures pulled out of the NVD (Dairy Foods and Airline Food Systems) made some NVD staff members somewhat reluctant to initiate closely related ventures.

At several companies, the NVD continued to launch closely related ventures despite pressures to spin them off-- usually because of a changing corporate strategy emphasizing closely related diversification. The result in at least two of these cases was a gradual process of evolution from a mission of "unrelated" diversification to a mission of "related" diversification to being redefined as a staff function. The evolution of Standard Chemical's NVD followed this pattern as is documented in figure 7-8.

Year	Mission

1968   "Get into anything but chemicals"

1971-1972   "We decided we were going too far out and that we were overlooking plenty of opportunities closer to home."

1973   "I re-wrote the charter and directed our efforts much closer to the businesses we were already in."

1974   "There was no expectation that I would initiate new ventures."

1975   "The NVD was redefined as a staff staff department. Its responsibilities included business planning, review of investment projects. . .and analysis of potential acquisitions for the divisions."

UNRELATED DIVERSIFICATION

RELATED DIVERSIFICATION

REDEFINITION

Figure 7-8. The Evolution of Standard Chemical's NVD

At another company, Consumer Products Corporation (disguised name), the evolution of the NVD also followed this pattern as shown in figure 7-9.

Year	Mission

1972   NVD started by the president. Its mission is to develop product concepts in new categories of business, test the product concepts, develop a business plan, and begin to sell the products.

UNRELATED DIVERSIFICATION

1974 .   NVD manager replaced. Mission shifts to pursuing ventures which build on Consumer Products Corporation's existing marketing capabilities. "The earlier ventures were farther departures from the company's existing lines than we now go after."

RELATED DIVERSIFICATION

1975   It is decided that the NVD's activities should end with the preparation of a business plan. "The NVD will no longer be involved in sales testing products. We don't have the budget or the personnel."

REDEFINITION

Figure 7-9.   The Evolution of Consumer Products Corporations NVD

In 1975, the NVD at Consumer Products Corporation was thus in the process of being redefined as a staff department.

INDIVIDUAL PERSONALITIES AND ORIENTATIONS

A fourth source of tension in the relationships between NVDs and other departments was one of personalities and orientation of individuals. This was not a major factor in the three case studies presented. However, in several staid and conservative companies, the NVD manager and venture managers were entrepreneurs and mavericks and this clash made cooperation and communication difficult.

One example of this is provided by a large, relatively bureaucratic manufacturing company, where the NVD manager was recruited from outside the company. He was a successful entrepreneur having built up a multimillion dollar business which he had sold prior to taking the position as NVD manager. He experienced difficulty in becoming acclimated to a large corporate environment and had difficulty relating to the typical corporate executive. His comments included the following:

"There is a real-world element missing in someone who has lived in a large corporate environment. In their world money comes out of a magic dispenser and this results in a different attitude toward spending. There is a big difference between using corporate money and using your own. . ."

"There is a very high amount of energy devoted to politics—discussing what other people are doing—instead of problem solving. . ."

"I found my boss indecisive. He had too many other concerns which prevented him from devoting sufficient attention to new ventures."

An individual who was familiar with the development of the NVD of this company (it survived only two years) attributed part of the problem to this "entrepreneur's" inability to work effectively in the environment of a large corporation.

IMPORTANCE/DIFFICULTY OF RELATIONS WITH DIVISIONS

The importance of good relations between the NVD and the operating divisions and the ease of achieving these appeared to vary with the type of NVD.

A MICRO NVD is dependent on operating divisions for support and "bootlegging personnel and facilities." In contrast, a MACRO NVD is more self-contained and can exist almost independently. Thus, good divisional relations are more important to the former.

They also appear to be more easily achievable for a MICRO NVD since it is considered less of a threat to divisional territory and not a serious competitor for corporate resources. Ralston Purina's NVD in its first few years and DuPont's NBO illustrate this point. They were both MICRO NVDs, dependent on the assistance of the operating divisions and able to obtain it with little difficulty. In contrast, DuPont's NVD in the sixties and Standard Chemical's NVD were MACRO NVDs. They had less harmonious relations with the operating divisions but had correspondingly less need for their cooperation and assistance.

Evidence of this is provided by the fact that the "emergence" of an NVD appeared to exacerbate relations with the operating divisions. The one example of emergence in the three cases studied, Ralston Purina, demonstrated this very clearly. In its early years, as a MICRO NVD, Ralston Purina's NVD was viewed as insignificant. It was tolerated and there was minimal resistance from other departments except for that which centered around specific issues such as the transfer price dispute with the Chow division. It was only when the NVD began to emerge--gain increased power, size and importance--that resistance to it mounted. This was finally partially countered when the NVD's positon in the organization was "moved down a notch."

MECHANISMS TO IMPROVE RELATIONS WITH OTHER DIVISIONS

In the companies studied, there were four mechanisms which appeared to contribute to better relations between the NVD and the operating divisions.

At DuPont Company, a Resource Board appeared to facilitate access to and the cooperation of operating divisions. The Resource Board membership was considered an honor and representatives were selected from the divisions which were to be drawn on for assistance and support. In addition to providing for better cooperation, it smoothed the spin off process when the venture was commercialized.

Two other mechanisms for improving relations between the NVD and operating divisions were employed by Hal Dean at Ralston Purina. When the NVD was losing the cooperation of the division, he made two changes. First he changed the organizational positioning of the NVD so that it no longer reported to him but was a notch lower in the organization. Secondly, he began to treat the NVD more even-handedly in meetings with other divisions. The effect of both moves was to free the NVD somewhat from its "crown prince" image and also to reduce the threat it posed in the competition for corporate resources.

A fourth mechanism which appeared to be instrumental in improving relations between the NVD and operating divisions was the evolution of DuPont Company's NVD from a MACRO to a MICRO NVD. As explained above, relations between a MICRO NVD and operating divisions tend to be smoother than those of a MACRO NVD.

Perceived Performance

The perceived performance of an NVD was a third factor (in addition to sponsorship and relations with other divisions) which appeared to influence its "political posture." As with any department, the way an NVD is viewed by both the operating divisions and top management is to a large exteent determined by its "track record." This ultimately affects the commitment of the NVD's sponsor, the relations with other departments and the objectives and ambitions which develop within the NVD itself. Favorable performance appeared to reduce the vulnerability of the NVD, yet it usually encouraged it to pursue a more ambitious course and made it possible to secure the necessary support to do so.[7]

At Ralston Purina, the NVD's successes in its early low-risk ventures (Dairy Foods and Industrial Protein) appeared to encourage it to "emerge" and pursue riskier, long-term ventures such as Mariculture and Mushrooms and to rapidly expand the Food Protein venture as well.

In contrast, the NVD's poor performance at Standard Chemical contributed to its eroding political position and the decision to modify its objectives. The less ambitious missions adopted by the NVD in 1973 and 1974 were not only proposed by the Executive Committee but resulted from lower aspirations within the department itself as well.

EXPECTATIONS GENERATED

It should be emphasized that the performance of the NVD is evaluated in relation to the expectations that have been generated and the objectives which have been set for it. High expectations appear to increase the likelihood of dissatisfaction with the NVD's performance.

In the cases of both Ralston Purina's NVD and DuPont's NBO, the department was established with a low profile and minimal expectations. In both cases, its performance was viewed favorably. This reflected both their actual performance and their performance in relation to the expectations generated.

In contrast, at Standard Chemical the NVD was established with high expectations. As one individual in the NVD commented:

> "The NVD was a hot area. It was in the limelight, featured in the company magazine, in annual reports and so on. The expectations generated were unrealistic."

Undoubtedly, these high expectations contributed to the erosion of support for the NVD.

The factors determining the perceived performance of the NVD are shown in Figure 7-10.

Sub-Unit Objectives

The fourth factor which appears to influence an NVD's "political posture" is the development of sub-unit objectives within the department. The evolution of an NVD was often characterized by the development of departmental objectives and ambitions which differed from its corporate mission or objectives. These usually expressed themselves as pressures for maturation--that is, for the NVD to retain the ventures it initiated.

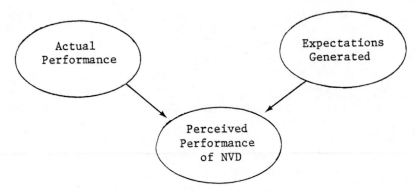

Figure 7-10. Perceived Performance of NVD

The extent to which sub-unit objectives (primarily for the retention of ventures) differing from the NVD's corporate mission arose appeared to be a function of the two factors shown in figure 7-11.

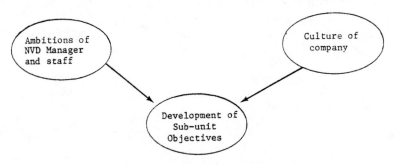

Figure 7-11. Sub-Unit Objectives

AMBITIONS OF NVD MANAGER AND STAFF

The various NVD managers and their staffs differed in their personal ambitions. DuPont's NBO and Ralston Purina's NVD posed a marked contrast in this respect. The former was populated mainly with commercial development men. They had been in the Development department for a decade or more starting ventures and spinning them off. Their personal values and ambitions were such that they preferred launching new ventures to operating going businesses. The NBO manager shared these values. In addition, he did not see his advancement within the company coming through the maturation of the NBO into an operating division.

The opposite was true at Ralston Purina. Win Golden was ambitious and aggressive. He used the NVD as a vehicle for personal advancement and in fact was lured to it because it was outside of the corporated hierarchy. The venture managers who reported to him were operations men--interested in managing on-going businesses as well as starting new ones. Neither Paul Hatfield nor Dennis Zensen had been in commercial development prior to joining the NVD. They similarly saw the NVD as an opportunity to leap frog the normal career path within the company.

CULTURE OF COMPANY

The culture of the parent company was the other factor which appeared to determine the extent to which sub-unit objectives developed within the NVD. Although it is difficult to describe or characterize a company's culture there were two aspects of the culture which seemed most relevant:

1. How launching ventures, as an activity in itself, was viewed.
2. How "empire building" was viewed.

Again, DuPont and Ralston Purina provide the best contrast.

At DuPont, launching ventures was valued as an activity in its own right. This can be attributed to the company's R & D emphasis and its historical growth through introduction of innovative products. At Ralston Purina, "new ventures" were not a part of the traditional activities of the company. There was little likelihood that Win Golden could have advanced in the company as a "commercial development man." In fact, this was one reason why he "received sympathy cards" from his friends when he took the job as NVD manager.

On the other hand, "empire building" seemed to be more a part of corporate life at Ralston Purina. When the NVD was set up in 1967, the company had developed into two large, bureaucratic "empires" - the Chow business and the Consumer Products business (primarily pet food). Thus, it was not surprising that Win Golden may have seen his future as building a third "empire." In contrast, DuPont was organized into a dozen operating divisions, all of which reported to the Executive Committee. The company had traditionally been managed by the Executive Committee as a group. There was substantial rotation of personnel between divisions at the middle management level and above and "empire building" was not a viable way to advance within the company.

It has been argued above that the ambitions of the NVD manager and his staff and the company culture determined the extent to which sub-unit objectives to retain ventures developed within the NVD's.

There appear to be three main reasons why these develop:

1. Empire building.
2. To provide a financial umbrella.
3. Personal involvement.

These are discussed below.

WHY SUB-UNIT OBJECTIVES DEVELOP

Empire Building

The norms and values of many large corporations typically place value on profitability, size and growth and encourage "empire building"-- personal advancement by presiding over or being a part of a sub-unit of the organization which is growing both in size and importance. An individual's status is enhanced by the size of his budget, the number of individuals reporting to him, the rates in which these are increasing, and similar measures relating to growth and size.

This appeared to be the case at Ralston Purina where Win Golden advanced in the ranks of the corporation as the NVD grew. When it reached sufficient size to be called a "group," he was promoted to Group Vice President. Although his performance in heading up the NVD may have been the primary reason for his promotion, his division's sales had to reach a certain minimum level before it could be called a "group."

To Provide a "Financial Umbrella"

To a varying degree in different organizations, a given division's access to resources is a function of its size and profitability. Within this system, NVD managers sometimes attempt to retain successful ventures to provide a "financial umbrella" for development of additional ventures. Retention of profitable ventures in the NVD appears to have a double-edged effect: it increases the NVD's self-sufficiency and it bolsters its position vis-a-vis the operating divisions in competing for the capital.[8] An NVD Manager at one company explained:

> "We need to grow ventures to provide an unbrella for our development work. In effect, we need profitable businesses within the NVD to finance us. If we are depending on other divisions within the company to provide our financing, it is likely that if our activities ever become significant, they will not support us. The alternative which we are following is to keep profitable businesses within the NVD and to become a mini-conglomerate."

The desire to have a financial umbrella for the NVD's development activities was a major factor in Win Golden's reluctance to spin off the Dairy Food venture to the Chow division. Hal Dean also mentioned this as one reason why he sided with the NVD in this dispute.

At DuPont Company, there was also an indication that the one venture which had remained in the NBO after being commercialized was serving as a "financial umbrella." A second, related development project had begun within it and one individual commented that it was also supporting a limited amount of development work on other ventures.

Personal Involvement

Individuals who had invested time and energy in launching a new business were often reluctant to have it leave their domain. The NVD manager at several companies stressed the impact of personal involvement with ventures. The following comment was typical:

> "It is not a natural cycle. To build something and be successful and then to give it up and do it over again is not a natural process."

At Standard Chemicals, there were pressures to retain ventures in the NVD. The Development Manager for the NVD commented:

> "Once a venture was going, I was reluctant to see it leave our area. I usually wanted to hold on to it at least a little longer."

In addition to empire building and the desire to provide a financial umbrella, personal involvement with ventures served as a third blockage to spinning off the ventures. Within the NVD, the venture managers became committed to their ventures, but also desired to remain in the NVD. This was a contributing factor to the NVD's maturation.

Summary

As shown in Figure 7-12, it has been argued that two clusters of factors are the major influences on the *direction* of evolution of an NVD (whether it "emerges" or "declines"):

		Direction of NVD Evolution	
		Emergence	Decline
Determinants of NVD Evolution	Corporate Strategic Posture	Diversifying	Consolidating
	NVD Political Posture	Building	Eroding

Figure 7-12:   Direction of NVD Evolution

The relationships between the corporate strategic posture and the NVD political posture and the direction of NVD evolution are central findings of this thesis. They enable one to develop the predictive and explanatory model, shown in Figure 7-13.

NVD Political Posture	Building		Emergence
	Eroding	Decline	
		Consolidating	Diversifying

Figure 7-13:   Model of NVD Evolution

An NVD in the bottom left quadrant will clearly experience strong pressures for its decline. Its political posture is eroding and the corporate strategic posture is one of consolidation. Both of these factors will tend to bring about its decline. Similarly, an NVD in the upper right quadrant will tend to evolve in the direction of emergence. Its political posture is building and the corporation is in a diversifying posture. If an NVD is in the bottom right or upper left quadrants, its direction of evolution is not immediately apparent from this chart. It will depend on the relative influence of the NVD's political posture and the corporation's strategic posture.

PART II. PATH OF NVD EVOLUTION

The first part of Chapter 7 has been a discussion of the factors which influence the *direction* of NVD evolution. This second part of Chapter 7 will focus on the "situational" factors which appear to have determined the specific *path* of evolution followed by each of the companies studied in-depth.

I will begin by reviewing and analyzing each of the three case studies presented earlier. This part of the chapter will then conclude with the identification of an apparent relationship between the mission of an NVD and its tendency to mature, be redefined or be eliminated.

ANALYSIS OF CASES

DUPONT COMPANY

DuPont provides an example of the decline of an NVD and its evolution from a MACRO to a MICRO type NVD.

1960's: MACRO NVD

The approach of the Development department in the 60's clearly identified it as a MACRO NVD. Its prime objective was to make an impact on the company. Thus it pursued large "frontal assault" ventures. The NVD developed venture ideas through a scanning and analysis of environmental trends and the identification of growth industries. These were entered through minority equity investments as well as start-up ventures. DuPont's Development department of the sixties is compared to the description of the "ideal type" MACRO in Figure 7-14.

	MACRO NVD	Development Department in the 1960's
SIZE/ OBJECTIVES	• Large scale • High profile and expectations • Objective: to make greatest impact on company	• "There was the hope and expectation that these ventures would have a major impact on corporate earnings." • "The number of staff people working on ventures grew from 12 to over 200."

Figure 7-14: Comparison of DuPont's Development (in the 1960's) and Ideal Type MACRO NVD

	MACRO NVD	Development Department in the 1960's
IDEA GENERATION	• NVD is venture idea generator • Idea originates as broadly defined business -- refined into specific products • Origin of idea: systematic scanning and analysis of environment	• "The department attempted to generate venture ideas by looking to the future to determine where there would be abnormal rates of growth and asking how could we get in these with our skills and technology."
VENTURES LAUNCHED	• Large scale • Multi-pronged entry including startup ventures, minority equity investments and/ or small acquisitions. • Frontal assault approach • Product line aimed at large market segment • Glamorous, high risk • Large front end investment/long term payoff	• "The typical venture launched by the Develp. Dept. in the 1960's was described by one individual as a large scale frontal assault on a new market." • "The program . . . consisted of two main thrusts: . . .minority equity investments in small, high technology companies and startup ventures." • "The size of the venture and its potential growth were key criteria for selecting ventures." • The Development Dept. was forced into areas which were even more speculative, taking on the riskiest least related products."

Figure 7-14: Comparison of DuPont's Development (in the 1960's) and Ideal Type MACRO NVD (Continued)

Through the mid-sixties, this MACRO NVD appeared to represent a "fit" with DuPont's corporate situation. The company had slack resources. Its earnings were on an increasing trend through 1965 and top management had adopted a strategy of diversification. The company's businesses appeared to be maturing and both historical precedent (an important factor in DuPont) and anti-trust considerations dictated the venture approach.

Change in Corporate Situation

As early as 1966, when the decade long uptrend in earnings was reversed, the corporate situation began to change. The changing financial picture and the company's disappointment with the ventures under way were the major driving forces behind the NVD's evolution.

The influence of the company's financial position on the NVD is apparent in the comment of the Executive Committee member who observed:

> "All we need is a little extra money to get into the bad habits of the sixties."

The critical change in the company's financial position and the resultant change in strategy occurred in the period 1969 to 1971. It was apparent from discussions with Executive Committee members that the recession in 1970 and the tightening cash situation were key factors in bringing about the "rigorous program to reduce costs and increase profitability" which was alluded to in the 1971 annual report.

The company's experience with the ventures launched in the early sixties was the second critical factor bringing about the decline of the NVD. It should be noted that the evolution of DuPont's NVD was influenced by both the performance of the Development department's own ventures and the performance of the broader company wide venture effort. Both of these resulted in top management disenchantment with the Development department's venture effort.

The most visible results of the corporate-wide venture program were several extremely large venture failures with combined losses of well over $100 million. The Development department had one very large venture failure and several others which were shut down early in their development. It was decided to divest all of the minority equity investments made by the Development department. In 1975, only one of the Development department's start-up ventures of the sixties was still intact. In fact, it was very successful and in retrospect considered by some to have justified the department's total venture effort.

In 1968, the first indication of a lessening of support for the NVD became apparent. The individual who headed up the venture effort from its inception was promoted to a position of division general manager. The individual who replaced him only remained in the position for about one year before being named an assistant division general manager and then later a divisional general manager. This high turnover at the top of the NVD appears to be a signal of the NVD's impending decline as this occurred at a comparable point in the evolution of Standard Chemical's NVD.

The years 1969 to 1971 were clearly the critical years in the changing corporate situation and it was during this period that the obvious misfit between the strategy of consolidation and a MACRO NVD became apparent.

Given this misfit, the pressures for the decline of the NVD were predictable.

Evolution into MICRO NVD

As can be seen in Figure 7-15, the NVD at DuPont evolved into a MICRO NVD with the establishment of the NBO in 1970.

WHY NOT REDEFINED OR ELIMINATED

An obvious question is "why was the NVD not redefined or eliminated at this point?" The following factors explain at least in part the NVD's evolution into a MICRO type rather than its elimination or redefinition. Perhaps most important was the company culture which valued venturing. As described earlier, the R & D orientation and historical growth through innovative products had resulted in the acceptance of the view that the company "should" be launching new ventures. As a member of the Executive Committee explained:

> "We are a research based company...Thus, we always want a stable of ventures."

The question in 1970 was thus "how large a stable of ventures should DuPont have?"

There are several other apparent reasons why the company avoided the more drastic steps. It was conservatively managed financially (with one of the strongest balance sheets in the industry) and could afford to move slowly and deliberately. Top management's leadership style was "democratic" rather than "directive." The Executive Committee made major decisions as a group and this "conscensus approach" tended to result in a balanced course of action--compromise and the avoidance of extremes. The Development department had other functions which could not be abandoned but would have had to have been parceled out. These included licensing technology, corporate

	MICRO NVD	NBO
SIZE/OBJECTIVES	• Small scale • Low profile and expectations • Supplementary role in implementing corporate strategy, often including trouble shooting • Objective: start successful ventures at least cost	• The NBO sought to develop ventures which represented recombinations or resynthesis of existing company resources and capabilities. • "The NBO is one of the charming things we have around." • The mission of the NBO was not to redirect DuPont or to make a substantial impact on its diversity.
IDEA GENERATION	• NVD is venture idea clearing house • Idea originates as specific product--develops into broader business concept • Origin of idea: Entrepreneur/inventor/product champion	• "The NBO did not carry out any internal idea generating or brainstorming but rather served as a clearinghouse for the ideas of others." • The department evaluated potential new business ideas that were generated both within DuPont and outside of it."
VENTURES LAUNCHED	• Small scale • Start-up ventures • Beach head approach • Single product aimed at market niche • Moderate risk • Small front end investment/ early breakeven	• "(We) run a meaningful market test at an early stage while trying to concentrate on not making any significant early capital investment." • "We now attempt to make a venture largely self-supporting early on." • The NBO attempted to launch small ventures targeted at a particular market niche." • "The NBO's activities were limited to start-up ventures."

Figure 7-15:   Comparison of DuPont NBO and "Ideal Type"
MICRO NVD

planning and internal consulting. The department was institutionalized and could not be as easily eliminated as a newly established NVD. Also, the disillusionment with venturing was not focused specifically on the Development department. It was responsible for only 20% of the company's ventures. Thus, the corrective action was not focused on the department but rather on the company wide program. Finally, when the NBO was established with its fundamentally different approach toward venturing, the department's activities once again became acceptable. The new approach of the NBO fit with the new corporate situation and reflected the decreased importance of venturing.

Summary

The evolution of DuPont's NVD can be explained in terms of the model presented earlier:

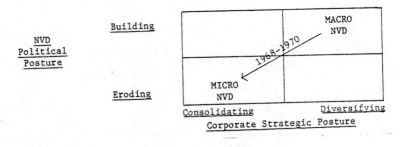

Figure 7-13: Evolution of DuPont's NVD

The key factor in the erosion of the Development department's political posture appeared to be disappointing performance of ventures - both the department's own ventures and those of the operating divisions of the company. The key factor in the changing corporate situation appeared to be the reduction in slack resources reflected in the tighter cash situation and the resultant shift to a strategy of consolidation. When the NBO was established as a MICRO NVD is re-established a fit with the new corporate situation as well as the political posture of the Development department.

STANDARD CHEMICAL

The Standard Chemical case provides an example of an NVD which became inoperative through redefinition. As with DuPont, both an erosion of its political position and the changing corporate situation were the major driving forces in bringing about its decline.

MACRO NVD

In 1968, the NVD was established as a MACRO NVD. This can be seen in Figure 7-16 which compares the "ideal type" MACRO NVD to that of Standard Chemical:

In 1968, the MACRO NVD fit with Standard Chemical's corporate situation. The outlook for the chemical industry both in terms of profitability and anticipated growth was becoming less favorable. Top management had thus adopted a strategy of diversification outside of the chemical industry and had given the NVD the task of implementing this strategy. Standard Chemical's president was a dynamic entrepreneurial individual and he strongly supported the NVD concept.

Change in Corporate Situation

However, in 1970 the corporate situation was changing radically. New opportunities emerged within the company's traditional lines of businesses. It became apparent that PVT and DAYLIN were going to experience tremendous growth. The capital demands of these two new products and the credit crunch developing in the economy put the company in a capital rationing position. With the retirement of Ken Anderson in mid-1970, top management's orientation changed as he was succeeded by more conservative individuals.

Erosion of Political Position

At the same time, the NVD's political position was eroding. Its "sponsor" retired, and perhaps even more important there was a growing disillusionment with the venturing concept. The modular housing venture was clearly failing and in its two years the NVD had not launched a single successful start-up venture. This track record was particularly disappointing when compared to the high expectations that had been generated.

Part of this erosion of the NVD's political posture had been built into it initially. The expectations generated were clearly too high. The lack of direction provided by the Executive Committee created a dilemma for Dr. Paulson. He could determine his guidelines only by bringing proposals before the Executive Committee. However, when these were repeatedly rejected, it weakened his position. His attempt to rectify this by seeking an appropriation of $2 million which would not

	MACRO NVD	Standard Chemical's NVD
SIZE/OBJECTIVES	• Large scale • High profile and expectations • Objective: to make greatest impact on company	• "(A) reason for establishing the NVD was a desire to diversify outside the chemical industry." • "The formation of the NVD was characterized by high exposure and high expectations." • "The NVD was guided by the objective of making a major impact on Standard Chemical in both sales and profit."
IDEA GENERATION	• NVD is venture idea generator • Idea originates as broadly defined business--refined into specific products • Origin of idea: systematic scanning and analysis of environment	• "Most ventures grew out of suggestions originating in the NVD." • "The approach was to have individuals in the NVD identify growth areas and make recommendations for how Standard Chemicals could participate in these markets." • "In most cases, venture ideas were derived from this systematic scanning, surveillance and analysis activity."
VENTURES LAUNCHED	• Large scale • Multi-pronged entry including start-up ventures, minority equity investments and/ or small acquisitions. • Frontal assault approach • Product line aimed at large market segment • Glamorous, high risk • Large front end investment/long term payoff	• "Size was an important criterion for selecting the ventures the NVD would initiate." • "The NVD attempted to take a several-pronged approach toward entering the selected areas including acquisitions, start-ups, and minority equity investments." • "There were pressures to produce large ventures that could contribute significantly to corporate earnings and sales."

Figure 7-16: Comparison of Standard Chemical's NVD (1968-1972) and Ideal Type MACRO NVD

be allocated to specific projects was rejected by the committee and further weakened his position. The lack of direction given Dr. Paulson and the difficulties this created provides a marked contrast to Win Golden's working relationship with Hal Dean at Ralston Purina.

Redefinition

The effect of the changing corporate and political situations upon the NVD were gradual. The style in the company was to move slowly and deliberately and there were other more pressing issues facing top management. However, over the four year period 1971-1975, the NVD slowly declined. The path of the NVD's decline was similar to that which was observed in other companies as well. A misfit developed between the mission of the NVD and the corporate strategy of expansion within existing business areas. This was initially reflected in pressures on the NVD to pursue more related ventures--those "closer to home." This, however, increased pressures to have ventures pulled out of the NVD earlier, because they were related to operations of existing divisions. Eventually the NVD became less involved in commercializing ventures and gradually assumed a staff function of searching for opportunities and developing business plans. This new role of the NVD eliminated the misfit between its mission and corporate strategy.

An alternate reaction to increased pressures to pull ventures out of the NVD is to pursue more unrelated ventures. This once again re-establishes the initial misfit and can result in elimination of the NVD. This dilemma which develops when corporate strategy changes is illustrated in Figure 7-17.

WHY REDEFINITION

There are several "situational" factors which appeared to have channeled the NVD in the direction of redefinition rather than elimination or evolution into a MICRO type NVD. First, the company's management style was to move conservatively. The group leadership in top management weighed in favor of a modification of the NVD rather than a more drastic step of eliminating it. Secondly, there was a new logical role for the NVD developing. The member of the Executive Committee to whom the NVD reported felt that the changes taking place in the chemical industry created the need for greater strategic analysis and planning. He felt there was a need to have a "staff arm" for the Executive Committee. Third, the individuals in the NVD were suited to this new role. They were to a large extent "planning people." The NVD had originally been staffed with several "futures oriented" staff people.

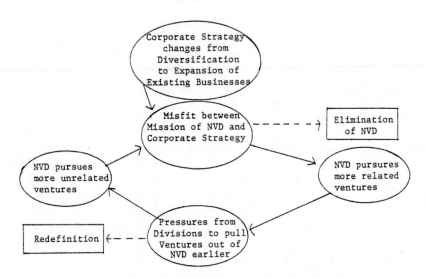

Figure 7-17: A Dilemma Due to a Change in Corporate Strategy

Summary

The evolution of Standard Chemical's NVD is summarized in Figure 7-18.

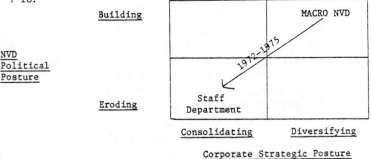

Figure 7-18: Evolution of Standard Chemical's NVD

MICRO NVD

In 1967, when the NVD was established, its charter read like that of a MACRO type NVD. However, Hal Dean and Win Golden recognized that given the period of transition the company was in and the questioning within the company of Hal Dean's strategy of diversification, a MACRO NVD might very well not survive to carry out its mission and at the least would create further divisiveness and tension. Thus, the NVD in reality began as a MICRO NVD. Its primary objectives during the 1967 to 1970 period were to build a track record of successful ventures and to develop "cash cows" to finance higher risk ventures which could have potentially greater impact. In Figure 7-19, the characteristics of the NVD during this period are compared to those of the ideal type MICRO NVD:

	MICRO NVD	Ralston Purina's NVD (1967-1970)
SIZE/ OBJECTIVES	● Small scale ● Low profile and expectations	● "Hal Dean's early instructions to Win Golden were: 'Pay your own way'."
	● Supplementary role in implementing corporate strategy, often including troubleshooting ● Objective:start successful ventures at least cost.	● "A low profile and pay as you go approach...served as key guidelines in Win Golden's planning." ● "The NVD was viewed as a relatively insignificant activity."
IDEA GENERATION	● NVD is venture idea clearing house ● Idea originates as specific product-- develops into broad- er business concept	● "Prior to 1970, the department's energies were focused on the on- going ventures which had been

Figure 7-19: Comparison of Ralston-Purina's NVD (1967-1970) and Ideal Type MICRO NVD

	MICRO NVD	Ralston Purina's NVD (1967-1970)
	● Origin of idea: Entrepreneur/inventor/ product champion	inherited or come about through trouble-shooting rather than being init-iated through a formal search ac-tivity."
	● Entrepreneur/inventor/ product champion	● "All ventures initiated by the NVD were either inherited with its formation, the a-doption of ideas which had been floating around the company or opportunistic ideas brought to an NVD member's attention."
VENTURES LAUNCHED	● Small scale ● Start-up ventures ● Beach head approach ● Single product aimed at market niche ● Moderate risk ● Small front end investment/early breakeven	● "We had always tried to test our ventures out on as small a scale as possible." "The early ef-forts of the NVD were aimed at developing new businesses with quick cash payout."

Figure 7-19: Comparison of Ralston-Purina's NVD (1967-1970) and Ideal Type MICRO NVD (Continued)

Emergence of NVD

During the next two years, (1970-1972) there were pressures to have ventures pulled out of the NVD early in their development. In the case of the Airline Food Systems venture, the operating division prevailed as it was quite clear that the venture was closely related to their existing business. As shown in Figure 7-17 if this continued it could have resulted in redefinition of the NVD. However, in the case of the Chow division's attempts to pull the Dairy Food Systems venture out of the NVD, Hal Dean stood firmly behind the NVD. This support combined with the decision within the NVD to pursue more unrelated ventures eliminated the threat of redefinition.

The key factors in the changing corporate situation were the growth of PVT and DAYLIN and the tightening financial picture. The erosion of the NVD's political position resulted from the failure of the modular housing venture, particularly in contrast to the high expectations generated for the NVD, and the departure of the NVD's sponsor.

RALSTON PURINA

Ralston Purina provides an example of the emergence of an NVD--its maturation from a MICRO type NVD to an operating division. In contrast to the DuPont and Standard Chemical cases where the corporate strategic posture appeared to be the major influence on the evolution of the NVD, at Ralston Purina the management of the NVD's political posture was the critical influence. The most interesting aspect of this case is that it illustrates the skillful management (by both Hal Dean and Win Golden) of the NVD's political posture. The NVD's sponsor, Hal Dean, varied his protection and support to balance the changing corporate situation, the changing relationship between the NVD and the operating divisions and the developing sub-unit objectives of the NVD. Win Golden was aware of the need to carry out a short term strategy of building a good track record and developing "cash cows" to support his longer term objective of making a major impact on the company. The effective management of the NDV's political posture allowed it to slowly but steadily emerge and mature. Of the three companies studied, this NVD appears to have been the most successful and to have had the greatest impact on the company.

The period 1972 to 1974, illustrates that if a MICRO NVD is to emerge to the point where it will significantly impact on the company, it is likely to encounter a major hurdle along the way. When the NVD begins to become significant in scope, it appears that resistance to it will increase. At Ralston Purina, this "hurdle" occurred in August 1972 when the NVD presented a plan to spend $60 million on the Food Protein venture over the next three years. This was the point at which the NVD was most vulnerable. Prior to that, it was rather insignificant and not worth fighting. After that, it had increased in size and power. This was also the point at which Hal Dean provided his strongest support. Without this support, it is doubtful that the NVD would have made it over this hurdle. It would have most likely remained small and insignificant or have succumbed to the pressures for redefinition or elimination.

A year later, the pendulum was swinging the other way. The emergency of the NVD was creating resistance and resentment among the operating divisions. Once again, Hal Dean reacted. He changed the reporting relationship of the NVD--"dropping it down a notch." He also lessened his visible support and favoritism for the NVD.

In 1974, when the company shifted temporarily to a strategy of consolidation, strong pressures against the emergence of the NVD developed once again. During the summer of 1974, Hal Dean held these at bay although allowing a significant cutback of the NVD's expansion plan. However, eight months later, when the corporate situation changed, he reacted immediately by allowing the NVD to resume its rapid expansion.

As described above, Hal Dean's careful management of his support of the NVD allowed this department to follow a course of gradual emergence.

Why Maturation

There are several apparent reasons why the NVD matured rather than evolved into a MACRO NVD. The most important factor was the orientation of the individuals involved. Win Golden was aggressive and ambitious. He saw the NVD as a means of making a major impact on the corporation as well as a vehicle for his own personal advancement. As the NVD grew in size, importance and prestige within the corporation, Win Golden rose within the ranks of its top management. When the New Venture Division became the New Venture Group in 1975, Win Golden advanced to the position of Group Vice President.

The orientation of the other individuals in the department supported these objectives. In general, they were not research, staff, or commercial development "types." Rather they were entrepreneurs and mavericks--operating men who saw the NVD as an opportunity to bypass the normal career path within the operating divisions and build their own empires. Thus, the personal objectives of the individuals in the department did not support the development of the MACRO NVD but rather led to the retention of ventures and the department's maturation into an operating division. In addition, both Win Golden and Hal Dean did not believe that a MACRO NVD would be supported within Ralston Purina. Throughout its development, their objective had been that the NVD be self-financing.

Summary

In Figure 7-20, the path of evolution of the NVD at Ralston Purina is illustrated:

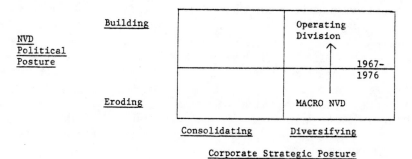

Figures 7-20:   Evolution of Ralston Purina's NVD

MISSION OF THE NVD AND PATH OF EVOLUTION

A central argument presented in this thesis is that the direction of NVD evolution is determined by the two sets of factors which have been discussed above--the corporate strategic posture, and the NVD political posture. The specific path of NVD evolution is determined by situational factors--those which are too varied and diverse to be generalizable across companies. Nevertheless, the relationship shown in Figure 7-21 between the mission of the NVD and the intensity of the pressure for maturation, redefinition, and elimination has been observed.

Mission of NVD \ Development Pressures For	Maturation	Elimination	Redefinition
Related Venture	Weak	Weak	Strong
Unrelated Venture	Strong	Strong	Weak

Figure 7-21:   Mission of the NVD and Pressures for Maturation,
Elimination and Redefinition

Maturation

The pressures for maturation are usually strongest when the NVD goes "far afield" in pursuing ventures which are perceived to be unrelated[1] to the parent company's existing businesses. It becomes less likely that there will be a division within the company which is anxious or even willing to take over the venture once it is commercialized. If it is not large enough to be spun off as a free-standing division, or if there is a decision to avoid proliferation of divisions (as in the case of Standard Chemicals), it will be retained indefinitely in the NVD. In DuPont, this tendency to retain "unrelated"[9] ventures was also apparent. The only venture which was likely to remain in the NVD indefinitely (or at least for several years after gaining market acceptance) was outside of the chemical industry, in a field which was perceived quite differently from any of the company's existing businesses. Similarly, at Ralston Purina the only venture spun off to a division was Airline Food Systems which was perceived as closely related to the Consumer Products Division's frozen food business.

Elimination

The pressures for elimination are likewise strongest when the NVD's mission is to launch ventures perceived as "unrelated" to the company's existing businesses. The greater the discontinuity and change in corporate strategy that the NVD represents, the stronger the pressures against it from conservative elements in management--often the Board of Directors, Executive Committee, and mature divisions. This may result in elimination, or as in the case of Standard Chemicals, Consumer Products Corporation, and other companies, the NVD's mission shifts to one of pursuing ventures perceived as more closely related to the company's existing businesses. The patterns of the NVD's evolution at Standard Chemical and Consumer Products Corporation, outlined earlier in Figures 7-8 and 7-9 illustrate this.

Redefinition

The pressures for redefinition appear to be strongest when an NVD pursues related ventures--ventures which are perceived to be closely related to one (or more) of its existing businesses. At DuPont, the manager of the NBO commented:

"The pressure to turn (a venture) over is greatest when there is a close fit with an operating division."

Similarly, one member of Standard Chemical's NVD observed:

"When you stay closer to home, the operating departments have more to say and there is increased pressure for ventures to be transferred out of the NVD."

When the fourth general manager of the NVD at Standard Chemical took over and was considering the role of the department, he concluded that the company should "not stray too far from what we do best" and that the operating divisions could launch these "related" ventures. Thus, he believed, that the role of the NVD should change "in the direction of planning...and it should get out of the business of running ventures." Quite clearly, the "relatedness" of the ventures to be pursued affected his thinking as to the role of the NVD. Specifically, since related ventures were to be pursued, this activity could be carried out by operating divisions, and the NVD should be redefined as a staff department.

Although the developmental pressures appear to be related to the mission of the NVD as shown in Figure 7-21 and described above, the mission of the NVD is only one of the numerous factors which affect the NVD's evolution. Thus it is not argued that the NVD's *path* of development can be predicted. In fact, there are several instances in which NVDs launching unrelated ventures were redefined and NVD's pursuing related ventures were eliminated. Nevertheless, although these pressures (which are related to the mission of the NVD) can be dominated by other factors, they are significant influences on the evolution of an NVD, important to managers interested in understanding and possibly controlling the changing role of an NVD within a company.

NOTES

[1] Andrews (1971).

[2] March and Simon (1958), p. 187.

[3] Cyert and March (1967).

[4] March and Simon (1958), p. 183.

[5] Zaleznick (1966), pp. 172-193.

[6] Bower (1972). See especially pp. 57-82.

[7] This is supported by March and Simon's (1958) contention that satisfactory performance tends to increase aspiration levels. See especially Chapter 3.

[8] The political nature of the competition for Funds had been documented by Bower (1970) and Wildavsky (1964).

[9] The terms "related" and "unrelated" as used in this discussion refer to management's perceptions (i.e., Do the Managers involved perceive a venture being related to an existing division's business?).

CHAPTER 8

IMPLICATIONS FOR MANAGERS AND RESEARCHERS

Chapter 8 will deal with the implications of this thesis for both managers and researchers. In the first part of this chapter, I will address the question of how the evolution of an NVD can be planned for, controlled, and managed.

In the second part of the chapter, I will discuss the implications of this thesis for the field of general management and offer several suggestions for future research.

This chapter differs from those preceding it in that I am attempting to go beyond the findings of the thesis to make recommendations to managers and researchers. Some of the points I will make will be supported by data while others are simply personal assessments and opinions which appear to be logical and probable. I will explain my rationale for these opinions but they are clearly open to challenge. In fact, they are presented in part to focus attention on certain suspected relationships and hopefully to stimulate discussion and further research.

It should be noted that many of the "implications" in this chapter are unsubstantiated by the data presented and less certain than the "findings" of the previous chapter. For the sake of style, the tentative nature of these statements is not continually restated.

THE NEED TO MANAGE NVD EVOLUTION

Why NVD's Fail

A key observation I made in the course of this research is the following:

> In the companies studied, the primary reason for "failure" of NVD's did not appear to be ineffectiveness in new business development. An NVD was an effective structure for managing new ventures in many companies. The main reasons NVD's became inoperative were that (1) the corporate strategic situation changed and the NVD was no longer needed, and/or (2) the NVD's political position eroded within the company and it was rejected by the existing power structure.[1]

This observation that in the companies studied, changes in the strategic and political situations appeared to be the dominant reasons accounting for the failure of NVD's (rather than ineffectiveness in managing new business development) should be of paramount importance to managers.   It suggests that a key to making an NVD successful lies in learning how to manage its evolution - its adaptation to changing corporate strategic and political situations.

Proactively Manage NVD Evolution

It was apparent in the companies studied that the need for an NVD varied as the corporate strategic situation changed. In some cases, the corporate strategy, the industry situation, the company's financial position and/or its leadership changed over a period of years so as to make it no longer desirable to have an NVD. In other cases, the need for an NVD remained or increased. In either situation, it is important to consciously and proactively manage the NVD's evolution. There are several reasons for this.

First, and NVD appears to be more fragile and vulnerable than other organizational sub-units. If management's objective is to retain the NVD over the long term (perhaps through several business cycles), it is important to have a long-term plan of vision for its evolution to prevent the NVD from being eliminated or redefined due to temporary "disturbances" (such as short-term cash crunches, periodic fads, or temporary overcapacity or undercapacity situations in an industry) or changes in its internal political situation.

For example:

> At one of the eighteen NVDs where interviews were conducted, an NVD was established in early 1974. Less than a year later, the company shut down one of its operations (which had been operating at a loss) and incurred a non-recurring loss of approximately $100 million. The "shock-waves" brought about a short-lived cutback in expenditures and the decline and redefinition of the NVD although the need for the NVD appears to remain.

If top management had a long-term vision for the NVD's development which included consciously attempting to insulate it from temporary shocks and distrubances, the NVD may not have been redefined. Rather it may have continued uneffected or more likely, it would have been temporarily cut-back with a clear commitment for its revitalization.

A second reason for proactively managing an NVD's evolution is that the different paths along which an NVD can evolve are not equally desirable in a given situaton. By predicting the direction of NVD evolution and taking certain steps (which will be outlined below) management can channel the NVD along the preferred evolutionary path. In some cases this would provide for the NVD's survival; in others, it might be desirable for the NVD to be redefined or eliminated.

This conscious channeling of the NVD's evolution can be extremely important as was illustrated by the DuPont case:

> When the MACRO venture activities of the Development department were declining in the late sixties, management set up a new MICRO NVD - the NBO. This provided for a continuation of venture generating activity. By taking this step, management introduced a different approach, one that appeared to fit with the new corporate situation and allow the NVD to survive.

A third reason for actively guiding and NVD's evolution is that as an NVD's profile increases and its demand for corporate resources grows, resentment and resistance toward it tends to develop. This "hurdle" can block its further emergence if it is not recognized and counteracted in some way. The best example of this was provided by Ralston Purina's NVD:

> As the NVD was maturing, perceptions of it changed and it encountered resistance from the operating divisions. At this point in its development, the NVD required strong support which was provided by top management. The further maturation of Ralston's NVD may have been blocked for several years, if not indefinitely, had this timely support not been provided.

Finally, it is important to proactively manage an NVD's evolution to avoid an unproductive, painful period of transition as the NVD gradually evolves into a fit with a new corporate strategic situation or a new internal political situation. When the NVD's mission represents a "misfit," there are tensions and pressures for change. If the NVD's evolution is effectively managed, these can be constructively channeled and focused in a clear direction. If it is not managed, they result in misguided efforts, wasted time, frustration, and frequent changes in objectives and approach. The Standard Chemicals case illustrates this point:

> During the period 1971-1975, there was a tremendous waste of time and energy as the NVD gradually evolved without direction into a new fit with a corporate strategic situation that had changed. For those four years, there was a high turnover of NVD general managers. The department was without a clear mission or direction to focus its work. Its efforts were scattered in several different directions and morale suffered.

Summary

It has been argued above that an NVD's evolution should be planned for and controlled. I am suggesting that both corporate top managements and NVD managers broaden their frame of reference - that they recognize that (1) there are quite different paths along which NVD's can evolve, (2) these are not equally desirable, and (3) management can and should determine which of these paths is followed. How this can be done is the subject of the section that follows.

MECHANISMS FOR CONTROLLING NVD EVOLUTION

The preceding chapters have described the ways that NVD's evolve and the factors that determine this. It is apparent that many of these factors are beyond management's control (for example, the outlook for an industry) and others certainly would not be modified for the sake of an NVD's development (i.e., corporate strategy). However, there are several variables which are under management's[2] control and can be used as levers or "mechanisms" to influence an NVD's evolution. Ten of these "mechanisms" are listed in Figure 8-1.

1. Varying top management support for the NVD
2. Changing the organizational positioning of the NVD
3. Selecting the staff of the NVD
4. Specifying criteria for the screening of ventures
5. Establishing intergrating mechanisms for the NVD
6. Creating a new NVD
7. Assigning additional functions to the NVD
8. Modifying the level of expectations for the NVD
9. Deciding the timing of venture spin-offs from the NVD
10. Modifying the NVD charter

Figure 8-1: Mechanisms for Controlling NVD Evolution

Top Management Support

Varying the amount of top management support for an NVD is a key mechanism for influencing its evolution. In general, by increasing its support for an NVD management can encourage its emergence and by decreasing its support, it can bring about its decline. It is important to recognize, however, that in some instances, too much support can bring about the decline of an NVD.

Top management support can take different forms and can be reflected in various ways. For example, top management can support the NVD by increasing the size of the NVD budget, by subsidizing it indirectly with other departments' budgets, by supporting NVD proposals, by praising it in group meetings, or by siding with the NVD in conflicts that arise.

How this support is provided to the NVD is critical. If it is interpreted within the company as clear favoritism, it can be counter-productive - that is, it can acerbate the NVD's relations with other divisions in the company and lead to its decline.

Too much support for the NVD can similarly undermine the NVD's political position. Both top management and the NVD manager should be sensitive to the need for balance. They should attempt to avoid or play down indications of favoritism and/or reduce the level of support for the NVD if resentment appears to be developing. In establishing growth objectives for the NVD they should take into consideration its expected future demand for resources and the anticipated response of the operating divisions.

Increasing support for the NVD can also lead to its decline if the NVD is "drowned" in excess resources. Although slack resources are required for innovation, constrained resources force creative problem-solving. With too much support, an NVD can suffer from too few demands for the effiecient utilization of its resources.

Organizational Positioning

The organizational positioning of an NVD is a second way in which management can influence its evolution. Changing an NVD's position in the organization signals changes in top managements' support. Raising the NVD's level in the organization indicates an increase in support and vice versa. As explained above, this can encourage either emergence or decline.

A second effect of an NVD's position in the organization is that it influences top management's involvement with the department.

In a MACRO NVD, where the department is expected to have a significant impact on the company, it is important to have top management actively involved in generating and screening ideas. This is one way to avoid the vicious circle of "NVD proposing/Executive Committee rejecting" which was seen in the Standard Chemicals case. In contrast, in MICRO NVD's, it appears that considerably less top management involvement is warranted. There are several reasons for this. First, venture ideas that develop are likely to be more specific than in a MACRO NVD and thus require more detailed and technical knowledge for their evaluation (i.e., "Is this sub-surface irrigation tubing a viable product?" versus "Should we commit resources to entering the Modular Housing industry?") Secondly, the ventures are not expected to consume substantial resources. Finally, there is the risk that innovative ideas will be rejected as "too far out" or "too risky" if top management is involved in their early development.

Thus, it appears that in general, MACRO NVD's should be positioned high in the organization and MICRO NVD's somewhat lower. Inappropriate positioning of an NVD can be detrimental to its performance and ultimately bring its decline.

Staffing

Staffing of the NVD is a third mechanism which top management can use to influence its evolution. It should be pointed out, however, that although staffing an NVD with a certain type of individual clearly influences its evolution, it is not argued that this mechanism alone will channel it along a particular path. Three important considerations in staffing an NVD are the orientation of the individual (their interests and ambitions), their capabilities and how they are perceived in the company.

Several suggestions of how an NVD's evolution might be influenced by its staffing are provided below:

Commercial Development Men

A high proportion of commercial development men in an emerging NVD may lead to the development of a Macro NVD rather than maturation. Commercial development men who have specialized in launching ventures and have a preference for that activity tend toward spinning off ventures once they are commercialized and in continuing to initiate and launch new ventures.

Aggressive Line Managers

On the other hand, staffing the NVD with aggressive line managers would probably be more likely to lead to maturation. Individuals with experience in line management and ambitions to advance in the corporate hierarchy tend to want to retain ventures they have launched. As was illustrated in the Ralston Purina case, this can create pressures for maturation.

Outside Entrepreneur

If a declining NVD is headed by an entrepreneur from outside the company, it appears to be more likely that it will be eliminated rather than redefined.   There are two reasons for this.

First, it was seen at several companies that independent entrepreneurs had difficulty functioning effectively within the political environment of a large corporation.   These conflicts may produce pressure for the elimination of the NVD.

Secondly, entrepreneurs are not likely to want to head up a staff department.   They are most often motivated by power and influence. This orientation tends to block redefinition without a change in personnel.

Staff Men

· Staffing an NVD with corporate planners and futures' oriented staff men can build in a tendency towards redefinition if the NVD declines.   Within the company, these individuals are already perceived as having the necessary experience and capabilities to carry out a staff function.   This was illustrated in the Standard Chemicals case where the staff-oriented composition of the NVD appeared to be a factor in bringing about its redefinition.

Divisional Veterans

An NVD can be staffed so as to facilitate the utilization of available resources within the company and encourage the development of a MICRO type NVD.

One way of accomplishing this is to staff the NVD with long-time company employees who have worked in several different divisions. They usually have a valuable network of contacts who can be drawn upon.   An alternative approach is to staff the NVD with representatives from various divisions and departments in the company.   Again, this establishes a useful intracompany network.

To summarize, the staffing of the NVD, both when it is established and during its development, can exert an influence on its evolution and thus serve as a mechanism for management control.

Criteria for Ventures

Specifying certain criteria for the screening of ventures is a fourth mechanism which management can use to influence the evolution of an NVD. Two particular criteria for screening ventures are important influences on NVD evolution:

Relatedness

The relatedness of ventures pursued by an NVD appears to have two main effects on its evolution. It effects the liklihood of success for the ventures and thus the NVD's political position and it also influences the pressures for maturation, redefinition· and elimination.

Managers face a dilemma in establishing criteria for the "relatedness" of ventures to pursue. Closely related ventures have the highest probability of success as the company will already have much of the required capabilities, knowledge, and experience. However, closely related ventures are often perceived as infringing on operating divisions' territories, creating conflict and producting pressures to have ventures spun off from the NVD early in their development. This may lead to redefinition of the NVD.

Pursuing more unrelated ventures may also create problems. Unrelated ventures will usually result in a higher proportion of failures. (The reasons for this are discussed later in the chapter.) Also they are likely to provoke opposition from conservative elements within the organiztion as they represent a greater departure from the company's traditional strategy. If successful, however, unrelated ventures tend to lead to maturation. Since there is no logical "home" for an unrelated venture, there will be little pressure to have it spun-off.

To summarize, by determining the "relatedness" of the ventures to be pursued, management can channel an NVD toward redefinition (related ventures) or maturation or elimination (unrelated ventures). However, management must also weigh the likely impact of "relatedness" on the NVD's performance.

Risk/Return Profile

The riskiness of ventures and the timing of their expected contribution are criteria of critical importance to an NVD. In this respect, an NVD's portfolio of ventures could be compared to a securities portfolio. The mix of low risk ventures with relatively short-term payback and longer-term high-risk ventures is a variable which management can use to influence the NVD's political position and the direction of its evolution. It is of critical importance that both the NVD manager and top management understand how this mix will influence the NVD's political posture.

A common mistake which can bring about the decline of an NVD is having a portfolio composed entirely of long-term high-risk ventures. If an NVD does not have shorter-term less-risky ventures in its portfolio, it will probably become a financial drain on the corpration and may not survive long enough to succced in its long-term venture efforts. Thus, short and medium term strategies are usually required for an NVD to fulfill its long-term objectives. A critical aspect of these strategies is the risk/return profiles of the ventures to be pursued.

Integrating Mechanisms

Establishing intergrating mechanisms which allow the NVD to draw on the resources of other units in the company is a fifth mechanism which management can use to influence NVD evolution. These integrating mechanisms can be in the form of informal personal linkages (such as staffing the NVD with long-time company employees or representatives from various departments which have key resources), formal organizational structures such as DuPont's "resource board," or the active involvement of a manager as an integrator.

The existence of integrating mechanisms is a key variable which will determine whether an NVD tends to be a Macro type or a Micro type. Where these are lacking, the NVD will have difficulty tapping into the resources of other departments. In this case, it may develop its own internal capabilities (even where these duplicate capabilities existing in other parts of the company) and evolve toward becoming a MACRO type NVD.

Integrating mechanisms also facilitate the spin-off of ventures to operating divisions. If a division which will be the recipient of a venture becomes involved in its management and planning during its early development, the eventual transfer is likely to be smoother and easier. On the other hand, lack of integrating mechanisms can be a blockage to the spin-off of ventures and encourage the maturation of an NVD.

Creating a New NVD

The creation of a new NVD appears to be a very effective mechanism for facilitating the evolution of a Macro NVD into a Micro NVD.

The DuPont case study illustrated this. In 1970, the Director of the Development department took the key step of creating the NBO. Had the NBO not been established, the Development department might very well have been redefined.

A key advantage that creation of a new NVD offers is the totality of change that can be brought about. For example, the difficulty of managing the decline of a MACRO NVD into a MICRO NVD is partly due to the fact that these two types of NVDs are so different with respect to the types of individuals they are staffed with, their relations with other departments, their relationships with top management, their philosophies and approaches. The difficulty of attempting to change all these elements within the same department are obvious. The creation of a new department thus appears to be an excellent solution to this problem.

Creating a new NVD seems to have promise as a mechanism for bringing about other changes as well. For example, earlier it was suggested that the staffing of an NVD influences the path of its evolution. Creation of a new NVD can be an effective way to introduce new people and a new orientation where it appears to be warranted.

It is also a way of avoiding an undesirable result which often accompanies elimination - that the NVD concept becomes discredited. For example, at one company where the NVD had been eliminated two years earlier, a former department member observed:

> "Today the word "venture" is taboo. Even if you have a venture, you don't call it that."

The creation of a new NVD to replace a declining one (perhaps one of a different type or with a different mission) appears to be one way to avoid the opportunity costs of having the venture concept discredited.

Additional Functions

Modifying the responsibilities of the NVD either by adding additional functions or taking away functions already performed by the NVD is another mechanism for channeling its emergence or decline along a specific path. Ironically, adding a function to an NVD can facilitate its decline (even though increasing its personnel and budget) if it shifts its primary function away from venture generation and commercialization towards staff activities. This was seen in the Standard Chemical's case. When the NVD was given responsibility for market assessment and planning of advanced research, although it increased its staff and budget, it was a step toward its redefinition.

Other examples of how adding or taking away NVD functions can influence its evolution are:

> 1. Adding a small, profitable on-going operation to the NVD (either spun-off from an operating division or acquired from outside the company). In addition to moving the NVD toward maturation by increasing the proportion of time spent to manage on-going businesses, the NVD will become less of a drain on corporate earnings.

2. Shifting staff responsibilities such as enviromental analysis or long-range planning to the NVD. This will push it along the path of redefinition.

In considering whether to give the NVD additional responsibilities, management should consider the fact that different functions often have quite different logics and create different managerial demands. To be managed effectively, they thus may require different types of managers, organization, and administrative systems. The fact that there was not a single NVD (of the sample of eighteen studied) which could be considered successful in start-up ventures, acquisitions, and minority equity investments suggests that it is difficult for a single department to manage these three different activities.

Expectations

The level of expectations which is generated for an NVD, either when it is initially established or during its development, can create strong pressures for its emergence or decline. In general, high expectations appear to result in pressures for decline while low expectations can facilitate an NVD's emergence. Excessively high expectations are obviously more of a problem with MARCO type NVD's than with MICRO NVD's.

Two factors contribute to the detrimental effects of high expectations. First, the higher the expectations which are generated for an NVD the more likely is disappointment with its actual performance. Generating initial high expectations can build in a "time bomb" - ultimately leading to redefinition or elimination. This was observed at Standard Chemicals and at several other NVD's as well.

The second effect of high expectations is that it creates pressures for the NVD to spend money and move ahead on ventures faster than may be prudent.

This appears to have been the case with Standard Chemical's Modular Housing venture. It was observed by one participant that one reason for launching the venture on such a large scale was that pressure had developed for the NVD to "produce an elephant not a mouse."

The problem of spending heavily early-on is two-fold. Investment in fixed assets limits a venture's flexibility and ability to adapt as it gains experience. Secondly, when NVDs spend heavily initially, they tend to "burn themselves out"--that is, their results cannot keep pace with their expenditures and the latter are cut back, often drastically.

Because it is difficult, if not impossible, for a MARCO NVD to maintain a low profile and low expectations, there are built in pressures for its decline. Thus, although a MARCO NVD will have a greater short-term impact on a company than a MICRO NVD, in the long term the latter may have a greater impact.

There are two ways this can be achieved. First, a MICRO NVD can pursue "exponential growth" - that is, it can encourage its sucessful beach-head ventures to launch second generation ventures, and those in turn to launch third generation ventures.

A second way for a MICRO NVD to have a major long-term impact is through its emergence. Its low profile and expectations appear to allow it to emerge "unnoticed" during its first few years. This gives it the opportunity to develop expertise in launching ventures, build a credible track record, and develop "cash cows" to finance its continued emergence.

Timing Venture Spin-Off

The timing of venture spin-offs is one of the most powerful mechanisms that management can use to influence and NVD's evolution. Nevertheless, in the 18 companies studied, there was a surprising lack of awareness of the importance, impact, and implications of venture spin-off decisions.

The timing of venture spin-offs is a very common area of conflict between NVD's and operating divisions and one which in almost all cases is referred to top management for resolution. It is thus of paramount importance to have a well thought out policy in this area.

There are two ways that this mechanism can influence NVD development. First, if ventures are repeatedly spun off early, the NVD will probably tend toward redefinition. Its activities involve a greater degree of investigation and planning and less actual involvement in the commercialization or operation of ventures.

On the other hand, if the NVD is allowed to retain ventures after their commercialization, it will eventually mature into an operating division. Attention will be focused on the management of on-going ventures to a greater degree than the generation of new venture ideas in their commercialization.

Management can thus influence NVD evolution directly either by formulating a set policy with respect to the timing of venture spin-offs and/or in adjucating the particular conflicts which arise.

NVD Charter

The initial composition and subsequent modifications of the NVD charter can be mechanisms for channeling the department along a specific path of evolution.   Two ways of doing this are to provide operating guidelines (such as specifying decision rules for the timing of venture spin-off or to set criteria for the selection of ventures) or to state a particular mission for the NVD. An example of the latter would be to assign additional functions to the NVD. Thus, the NVD's charter is a means for employing other mechanisms discussed earlier in this chapter.

> 1.   The Ralson Purina case illustrates this. In the NVD's charter, it was explicitly stated that the NVD should recommend the timing of venture spin-offs. This was one factor which allowed the NVD to retain ventures and ultimately mature.

> 2.   At Electronics Corporation of America (see Appendix 3-1), the NVD's charter specified a formula for the initial capitalization of ventures. It was based on a total capitalization of $200,000. Given this charter limiting the size of its ventures, the NVD was not likely to evolve into a MACRO NVD.

Because of its comprehensive nature - incorporating several mechanisms which influence NVD evolution, an NVD charter is a mechanism which is both powerful and complex. In most companies, its implications and effects are neither well understood nor given sufficient attention.

A second important point regarding an NVD charter is that it can and should be used as a mechanism to manage the NVD's evolution, rather than simply providing formal recognition of changes that have already taken place. In most companies studied, it was only modified to take formal after the fact recognition of changes. Typical examples of this were Standard Chemical's new charters in 1973 (to pursue related ventures) and in 1975 (to serve as a staff department).

BROADER IMPLICATIONS AND SUGGESTIONS FOR FUTURE RESEARCH

In the first section of this chapter, I have described the mechanisms which can be used to control the evolution of an NVD. It should be recognized, however, that in a system as complex as a large corporation, there are few simple cause and effect relationships. The unintended consequences of action can be greater than those which are intended. Thus, the "mechanisms" or "levers" discussed above should not be applied mechanically.   Rather than being substitutes for managerial judgment and intuition, they require judgement and intuition to be effectively utilized.

The remainder of this chapter will focus on three broad topics which are central to the field of general management:

1. Related versus Unrelated Diversification
2. The Evolution of Departments or Functions
3. Organizational Asymmetry

For each of these subjects, I will discuss the implications of this research and offer suggestions for future researchers.

Related versus Unrelated Diversification

The issue of related versus unrelated diversification has been a central topic in general management literature.   It has become widely accepted that companies are likely to be more successful in diversification efforts which are in areas closely related to their existing businesses as opposed to those efforts which are aimed farther afield.   Peter Drucker has argued that "the less diverse a business, the more manageable it is."[3] He has attributed this to the cognitive limits of managers - the difficulty of knowing and understanding several businesses.   He states:

> "When top management has to depend totally on abstractions, such as formal reports, figures, and quantitative data, rather than be able to see, know, and understand the business, its reality, its people, its environment, its customers, its technology, then a business has become too complex to be manageable."[4]

Two other prominent general management theorists, Kenneth Andrews and Igor Ansoff, have similarly advocated related rather than unrelated diversification.   Ansoff[5] has recommended "concentric diversification" into closely related businesses--specifically introducing existing products into new markets or developing new products for markets already served by the firm.

Andrews, in *The Concept of Corporate Strategy*, has challenged the conglomerate concept expressing doubts similar to Drucker's, as to whether conglomerates can be managed effectively over the long term.

Recent research by Richard Rumelt[6] has compared the performance of companies pursuing different strategies and has provided data in support of the views expressed by Drucker, Ansoff and Andrews.

Related versus Unrelated New Ventures

Comparing the performance of related and unrelated new ventures was not an objective of this thesis. Nevertheless, in the course of the research, I made observations related to this subject which may be of value to future researchers. Specifically, I have identified three reasons why related new ventures appear to be more successful than unrelated ventures.

The first reason is one which has been discussed by Drucker, Ansoff, Andrews, and others. When companies launch unrelated ventures, they often lack the requisite resources, capabilities, knowledge and skills. In contrast, when pursuing related new ventures (i.e., "concentric diversification" as recommended by Ansoff or "matching company capabilities with opportunity" as recommended by Andrews), there is a greater opportunity to transfer existing knowledge and skills.

A second advantage of more closely related new ventures is one which has not been discussed in general management literature. Related new ventures can be launched at lower cost than unrelated ventures. Thus, given an equal payback, the former will have a higher return on investment.

The key reason for this cost difference is that in launching a related venture, existing company resources can be expanded and drawn on (and often boot-legged) with only marginal added costs. In contrast, launching an unrelated venture usually requires a large front-end investment to build an infra-structure to support the venture. For example:

1.   At Standard Chemicals, the Lithomer venture could be launched at relatively low cost. There was an existing research program in photo-chemistry, pilot production facilities could be added to an existing plant, and many of the required raw materials were already produced by the company. The costs of the venture were mainly marginal costs of expanding staffing and facilities. Little fixed front-end investment was required.

2.   In contrast, Standard Chemical's Modular Housing venture required much higher investment. This was partly due to the nature of the product, but also reflected the fact that there was no existing infra-structure. Thus, a new plant had to be built from the ground up at a new site, development work could not be conducted in existing faciliities, and a new staff had to be recruited from outside the company (rather than borrowed on a temporary basis). This added substantially to the costs of the venture.

A third reason that related ventures appear to outperform unrelated ventures also has not been discussed in the literature.

Management commitment to and support for unrelated ventures tends to be fragile. It has been observed throughout this thesis that the NVD is one of the first places that management cuts back when resources become contrsained. Similarly, among new ventures, those which are least related are usually the first to be cut back.

Thus, not only do unrelated ventures have a higher cost and require greater learning than related ventures, they also tend to have less lasting support.

Summary

To summarize, it has been argued widely in general management literature that companies should stay with those businesses which fit their existing capabilities or venture into closely related areas. The main reason which has been offered for avoiding unrelated diversification relates to the skills and capabilities of the company--that the greatest likelihood of success is when these are matched with opportunities in the environment. In the discussion above, I have drawn on my observations of NVDs and suggested two additional reasons why unrelated new ventures are often unsuccessful: they are more costly and support for them is more fragile.

Future Research

In the past, researchers have sought to establish that companies pursuing related diversification outperform those with strategies of unrelated diversification. I believe that it is equally important, if not more important, to understand why this is so. One way of researching this would be to compare two competing businesses--one a division of a conglomerate and the other a division of a firm with a strategy of related diversification and attempt to relate their competitive strengths and weaknesses to the nature of their relationships with the parent organization.

The Evolution of Departments or Functions

One important difference between this thesis and earlier research on how companies organize for new business development, is that it is a "longitudinal study." That is, rather than describing or comparing organizations at a particular point in time, it has focused on how they have changed over an extended period, in this case, from eight to sixteen years. To my knowledge, there have been few if any earlier studies that have taken this "longitudinal" view of how companies organize for new business development.

This particular research approach allowed me to see a management dilemma which had been unrecognized by previous researchers, specifically, that NVDs typically had a long term mission but a short term life span. It also allowed me to identify the factors accounting for an NVD's short lifespan and how these can be controlled.[7]

Future Research

I believe that this research methodology could be used effectively to study the evolution of other corporate departments which have a long term mission. I would expect that departments such as Research and Development, Corporate Planning and Environmental Analysis have evolutionary patterns which are similar in some respects to those of NVDs and influenced by many of the same factors (i.e., the corporate strategic situation and the department's political position). One might hypothesize that these departments function as outlets for "slack" resources.[7] Thus, when the corporation is in an expanding/diversifying mode, they are expanded more rapidly than other departments while when the corporation is in a consolidating mode, they are cut back more drastically.

As with NVDs, most earlier research on Research and Development, Corporate Planning and Environmental Analysis has dealt with the management of these activities at a single point in time rather than their evolution. Nevertheless, an extremely important issue for both top management and middle-level managers is how to manage the evolution and development of these departments. I see this as an important area for future research.

Organizational Asymmetry

This thesis has addressed a very fundamental management dilemma: how to develop an organization which can effectively manage both new business development and mature or maturing businesses. It is well recognized[9] that new ventures and mature businesses differ with respect to their demands on management and the types of organization which they require. For example, new ventures and mature businesses differ with respect to their predictability, how they should plan, be funded and be evaluated, their objectives and time frame, and the organization structure, administrative systems, personnel and climate which they require.

It has been seen that the role of an NVD in the parent organization evolves over time, that shifts in its role often can be facilitated by management intervention and that its evolution is influenced by both the corporate strategic situation and factors influencing its political position.

The "NVD approach to managing new business development" could be considered an extreme example of "organizational asymmetry"-- differentiating divisions of a corporation so they are suited to the different types of businesses they are in. In almost any diversified firm, one sees less extreme examples of asymmetry--for example, at the simplest level, there is the asymmetry between high growth businesses and older, mature operations. As with NVDs, different types of divisions in a diversified firm evolve. High growth businesses mature, mature businesses begin to decline or perhaps enter a new growth phase, new families of products are introduced and new markets open up. One would expect that the evolution of different types of operating divisions in a diversified firm (i.e., to use a familiar terminology--"cash cows," "rising stars," etc.) has similarities to the evolution of NVDs and this would appear to be a fascinating subject for research. Among the research questions might be the following:

1. What are the patterns of evolution of "rising stars?"[10]
2. What influence does the corporate strategic situation have on the evolution of "rising stars?"
3. What kinds of problems, conflicts, tensions, or misfits result from the emergency or decline of "rising stars?"
4. In what ways can management control this evolution?

Summary

In the section above, I have discussed the implications of this thesis for the field of general management and suggested several topics for future research. Three main topics were discussed: related versus unrelated diversification, the evolution of departments and functions, and organizational asymmetry. I have pointed out and discussed three reasons why unrelated new ventures are less successful than related ventures. I have also suggested that the findings of this research which relate to NVDs are likely to be valid to some extent for othe departments with long range missions, for example, Corporate Planning, Environmental Analysis, and Research and Development. Finally, I have argued that NVDs are an extreme example of organizational asymmetry and that the evolution of different types of operating divisions in a diversified firm may have similarities to the evolution of an NVD. Each of these subjects has been suggested as a worthwhile area for future research.

NOTES

[1] The NVD's performance may be a contributing factor to the erosion of its political position but in many companies there were more important factors such as the NVD's sponsor leaving the company, excessively high expectations generated or the NVD appearing to pose a threat to other divisions.

[2] It will be apparent that some of these mechanisms are only available to top management while others are available to both top management and NVD managers.

[3] Drucker (1974), p. 679.

[4] Drucker (1974), p. 681.

[5] Ansoff.

[6] Rumelt (1974).

[7] Alfred Chandler's *Strategy and Structure in American Enterprise* is probably the best illustration of the power of longitudinal studies as a research methodology.

[8] See Cyert and March (1963) for a discussion of the concept of organizational "slack."

[9] See Burns and Stalker (1959), Hlavacek and Thompson (1973), and March and Simon (1958).

[10] One could substitute "cash cows," "dogs," or any other categorization of divisions for "rising stars."

BIBLIOGRAPHY

Andrews, Kenneth, *The Concept of Corporate Strategy*, Homewood, Illinois: Dow-Jones-Irwin, Inc., 1971.

Ansoff, H. Igor, *Corporate Strategy*, New York: McGraw-Hill, 1965.

Ansoff, H. Igor and R. G. Brandenberg, "A Language of Organizational Design," *Management Science*, August 1971.

Ansoff, H. Igor and John M. Stewart, "Strategies for a Technology Based Business," *Harvard Business Review*, November/December 1967.

Booz, Allen and Hamilton, *Management of New Products*, New York, 1963.

Bower, Joseph, *Managing the Resource Allocation Process*, Homewood, Ill.: Richard D. Irwin, Inc., 1972.

Buddenhagen, Frederick, *Internal Entrepreneurship as a Corporate Strategy for New Product Development*, Unpublished M.I.T. Masters Thesis, 1967.

Burns, Tom and G.M. Staulker, *The Management of Innovation*, London: Tavistock Publications, 1959.

Caves, Richard, *American Industry: Stucture, Conduct and Performance*, 3rd Edition, Englewood Cliffs, N.J.: Prentice-Hall, Inc., 1972.

Chandler, Alfred D., Jr., *Stragegy and Structure*, Cambridge, MA: The M.I.T. Press, 1962.

Collins, Gwyn, "The Management of New Product Development," *New Ideas for Successful Marketing*, Chicago: American Marketing Association, 1966.

Collins, Orvis and David Moore, *The Organization Makers*, New York: Meredith Corporation, 1970.

Cook, Frederic, "Venture Management as a New Way to Grow," *Innovation*, Number 25, 1971.

Cyert, R.M. and J.G. March, *A Behavorial Theory of the Firm*, Englewood Cliffs, N.J.: Prentice-Hall, 1963.

Drucker, Peter F., *Management: Tasks, Responsibilities, Practices*, New York: Harper & Row, 1974.

Drucker, Peter F., *The Practice of Management*, New York: Harper & Row, 1950.

Ehrlemark, Gunnar, "Running a Business versus Creating New Businesses," reprinted from a paper presented at a symposium on growth through acquisitions and divestments in Brussels, May 1974.

Glover, John D., *Rise and Fall of Corporations: Challenge and Response*, Harvard Business School case, 1967.

Griffin, John, *The Image of Innovation in Industry*, Unpublished Masters Thesis, M.I.T. 1969.

Haeffner, Eric, "The Innovation Process," *Technology Review*, March/April 1973.

Hanan, Mack, "Corporate Growth through Venture Management," *Harvard Business Review*, January/February 1969.

Hill, Richard M. and James D. Hlavacek, "The Venture Team: A New Concept in Marketing Organization," *Journal of Marketing*, July 1972.

Hlavacek, James, "Toward More Successful Venture Management," *Journal of Marketing*, October 1974.

Hlavacek, James D. and Victor A. Thompson, "Bureaucracy and New Product Innovation," *Academy of Management Journal*, September 1973.

Jones, Kenneth and David Wileman, "Emerging Patterns in New Venture Management," *Research Management*, November 1972.

Langrish, J. et al., *Wealth From Knowledge*, New York: John Wiley & Sons, Inc., 1972.

March, James Co. and Herbert A. Simon, *Organizations*, New York: John Wiley and Sons, Inc., 1958.

Markham, Jesse W., *Conglomerate Enterprise and Public Policy*, Boston: Division of Research, Harvard Business School, 1973.

Myers, S. and D.G. Marquis, *Successful Industrial Innovation*, Washington, D.C.: National Science Foundation, 1969.

Nevins, Alan and Hill, *Ford: Decline and Rebirth*, New York: Scribners, 1962.

Normann, Richard, "Organizational Innovativeness: Product Variation and Reorientation," *Administrative Science Quarterly*, June 1971.

Normann, Richard, *A Personal Quest for Methodology*, Stockholm: SIAR, 1973.

Roberts, Edward, "A Basic Study of Innovators: How to Keep and Capitalize on Their Talents," *Research Management*, July 1968.

Roberts, Edward, "What It Takes to Be an Entrepreneur -- And to Hang on to One" *Innovation*, Number 7, 1969.

Robertson, A.B. et al., *Success and Failure in Industrial Innovation*, Sussex, England: Center for the Study of Industrail Innovation, University of Sussex, 1972.

Rothwell, Roy, "Nucleonic Thickness Gauges - A SAPPHO Pair," *Research Policy*, Number 2, 1973.

Rothwell, Roy, et al., "SAPPHO Updated - Project SAPPHO Phase II," *Research Policy*, Number 3, 1974.

Rumelt, Richard P., *Strategy, Structure and Economic Performance*, Boston: Division of Research, Harvard Business School, 1974.

Schon, Donald, "Champions for Radical New Inventions," *Harvard Business Review*, March/April 1963.

Schon, Donald, *Technology and Change*, New York: Delacorte Press, 1967.

Schumpeter, Joseph A., *Capitalism, Socialism and Democracy*, 3rd Edition, New York: Harper & Brothers, 1950.

Scott, Bruce, "The Industrial State: Old Myths and New Realities," *Harvard Business Review*, March/April 1973.

Selznick, Phillip, *Leadership in Administration*, New York: Harper and Row, 1957.

Springborn, Robert, "An Entrepreneurial View of Entrepreneurship," *Chemtech*, May 1974.

Towers, Perrin, Forster and Crosby, *Venture Management*, New York, 1970.

Trevelyan, Eoin, *The Strategic Process in Large Complex Organizations*, Unpublished Doctoral dissertation, Harvard Business School, 1974.

U.S. Department of Commerce, *Technological Innovation: Its Environment and Management*, 1967.

Vesper, Karl H. and Thomas G. Holmdahl, "How Venture Management Fares in Innovative Companies," *Research Management*, May 1973.

Von Hippel, Eric, *An Exploratory Study of Corporate Venturing - A New Product Innovation Strategy Used by Some Major Corporations*. Ph.D. Thesis. Carnegie-Mellon University, 1973.

Weick, Karl E., The Social Psychology of Organizing, Reading, Massachusetts: Addison-Wesley Publishing Co., 1969.

Wildavsky, Aaron, *The Politics of the Budgetary Process*, Boston: Little, Brown & Co., 1964.

Wileman, David and Howard Freese, "Problems New Venture Teams Face," *Innovation*, Number 28, 1972.

Zaic, Gregory, *Success and Failure of New Ventures in a Small to Medium Sized Company*.

Zaleznick, Abraham, *Human Dilemmas of Leadership*, New York: Harper & Row, 1966.

APPENDIX 3-1

MICRO & MACRO NVD DESCRIPTIONS

The NVD in Electronics Corporation of America originated primarily as the idea and desire of the Chairman of the Board. He had two main reasons for establishing it: first, he believed there were entrepreneurs in the company and they might be lost if no "home" was provided for them within the company. In the past, the company had lost technical people who had gone into their own businesses. The primary aim of the NVD was thus to retain internal entrepreneurs. Secondly, he felt that the company should be diversifying into new businesses.

Early in 1972, the NVD was established. The most critical element in its design was an arrangement which permitted venture managers to have an equity position in their ventures. The typical venture was small, capitalized with $200,000. Eighty per cent was invested by the company, 10% by the Venture Manager, and 10% by a selected group of individuals in the company who wished to invest in the venture.

The objective of this arrangement was to offer the Venture Manager opportunities usually only available to an independent entrepreneur. It provided the venture manager with the opportunity to build his equity to $1 million or run the venture for twelve years, whichever came first. The company could then buy out the entrepreneur and investors and wholly own the business.

The NVD's main functions were described as "selling the concept of the venture program across the company, evaluating and screening ideas which were submitted (including providing limited resources to explore potential opportunities so that they would not be rejected arbitrarily) and managing the commercialization of the selected ventures."

The NVD's charter stated that it was not to pursue ventures which fell with the charter of an existing division and this disqualified several potential ventures. Ironically, although the aim of the NVD was to retain internal entrepreneurs, many of these were leaving the company to start businesses in direct competition with a product line of an existing division and thus could not be sponsored by the NVD.

The NVD set up a laboratory to assist entrepreneurs in evaluating their technical ideas and to facilitate the NVD staff's evaluation of their feasibility. In addition, there was a marketing staff in the laboratory to assist in developing a business plan and to provide other support activities.

Criteria for selecting ventures did not focus on particular industries or businesses although high technology, proprietary products were preferred. The NVD initially had to educate employees to what they were looking for. The NVD Manager explained:

> "We were looking for more than a listing of interesting areas like 'we should be in medical electronics.' We would reject those ideas out of hand. If you want to list a bunch of interesting fields, anyone can do that. We wanted to know what the entrepreneur could do differently from anyone else and why he thought it would be a success."

Three ingredients they sought in a venture were a "champion," a unique idea and a viable business plan. No ideas which were adopted as ventures were generated at the top of the organization. Most of the internally generated ideas came from the technical and engineering people and middle managers in the company.

A large number of ideas surfaced and were brought to the attention of the NVD. However, these were characterized as "product-ideas" not "new business opportunities." To be a business opportunity, "it had to have the potential to grow into a whole line of products to justify to the research, engineering and marketing investment."

The number of viable "business opportunities' generated from within the company was limited and thus the venture approach was modified and opened up to externally generated venture ideas. During the period 1972 to 1975, four small ventures were launched. They were not expected to have an impact on company earnings.

MICRO NVD DIVERSIFIED CHEMICAL COMPANY

The NVD in Diversified Chemical Company was established more than two decades ago. Its existence could be traced back to an early President of Diversified Chemical Company who instilled in the company a philosophy which stressed "the value of the individual". This philosophy and the corporate culture which emphasized venturing was reflected in the large number of new product ideas that were generated throughout the organization. The NVD Manager commented:

> "Almost every Diversified Chemicals employee thinks he can make a new product suggestion which someone will listen to."

The NVD manager felt that this belief was very important to the NVD's success. In addition, each research employee had 15% of his time allotted to work on his own project in the company's interest. It was noted that this was a myth in that usually the other 85% of their work expanded into a full time job. Nevertheless, almost all of the research employees had their own "pet projects" and substantial time was "bootlegged" to work on their own and others' projects.

The functions of the NVD at Diversified Chemicals were to evaluate, select, develop and commercialize venture ideas that were brought to its attention from within the company.

Project ideas originated at the bottom of the organization most often--that is, at the level of a bench researcher or a salesman. They then passed through a succession of screening levels in which they were evaluated. The NVD Manager explained:

> "We try to screen cheaply because the number of ideas is so great and a large percentage of our funds could conceivably be spent on screening."

Traditionally, the company had competed in relatively small market niches, selling a broad variety of products through several different sales forces. The NVD Manager observed:

> "Companies which like to dominate whole markets can't bother with the niches we go after."

Within Diversified Chemical operating divisions were very active in launching ventures. The NVD's activities accounted for a relatively small part of the company's total new business development efforts.

The primary criteria for selecting ventures were projected financial return and the venture's ability to gain support within the organization. There was no minimum size stated for a venture. One reason for this was that the "prospects for a business change so rapidly at the outset."

A technical staff reporting to the NVD Manager was responsible for the initial screening of projects. Each year approximately 1000 ideas were looked at and about 25 were considered seriously. At any point in time, about twelve projects were in an early development phase under the Technical Staff Manager, six projects were in the next level of screening, being carried as development projects under a Development Program's Manager, and about six projects were being commercialized as ventures.

Most ventures started small. The NVD Manager explained:

> "Our philosophy is to give an individual a little to begin with. If he is smart, he uses that to learn as much as he can to justify the next step."

There was a great deal of flexibility for a venture in its early stages and often if changed direction and aimed at a completely different market. The NVD Manager commented:

"We milk a technology to death."

The company's wide range of distribution channels facilitated access to a variety of markets.

Most of the venture managers in the NVD had moved laterally or downward to take their positions. A major reason they were willing to do this was that the traditional career path of Presidents, Chairmen and division managers in Diversified Chemicals had been to head up a successful venture and grow with it.

MACRO NVD CONSOLIDATED PAPER COMPANY

The NVD at Consolidated Paper Company was established in 1973. It was given the charter to "develop and execute strategies to get Consolidated Paper into new businesses."

The NVD was established for several reasons, most important of which were a desire to internally develop new businesses and a belief that the high R & D expenditures of the 1960s had produced few new products. The "guiding light" in sponsoring the NVD was the "number two man in the company," the General Manager of the largest division.

The NVD's functions included the generation of new venture ideas as well as managing their commercialization.

There were two venture--generating efforts in the NVD. One group of individuals attempted to identify markets for technological developments of the R & D department. The other group worked back from the company's marketing strength and consumer franchise (the Consolidated Paper name). This latter group conducted a "macro-screen" of all the products sold in a supermarket, identified all of the companies competing in products which could be of interest to Consolidated Paper and compared the competition's strengths to their own. Areas which potentially could be of interest included housewares, cleaning products and baby products.

Their criteria for ventures included the following:

1. Size - the venture must be a big business in order to impact on company profits. As a general rule it should have potential sales of $100 million in five to ten years.

2. Return on investment - the venture must have a projected return on investment which is higher than the corporation's overall goal.

3.   The venture must build on company strengths. These include timber resources, web-forming technology, existing consumer and industrial distribution channels, consumer products and advertising.

Typically, the ventures launched by the NVD were large. Three of the six ventures launched by the department had developed costs in excess of $10 million.

Originally, it was planned that they would enter new businesses solely through internal development.   However, as they screened businesses, they realized that internal development would not be possible for many businesses in the time frame they were considering.   Their approach thus broadened to include joint ventures and acquisitions.

MACRO NVD UNITED STATES CHEMICAL COMPANY

The NVD at U.S. Chemical Company was established in 1967. Its charter was to "go into business areas outside of those of the division."   One of its main tasks was also to commercialize developments of the Central Research organization which were not of interest to the operating divisions.   The "major force" pushing for establishment of the NVD was the Group Vice President for Technology.

New business ideas were generated by a Development Projects deparment within the NVD.   The search process was guided by formal corporate objectives providing directional guidance from the level of the Board of Directors.   The NVD Manager explained.

"They tell us what areas we want to be in--defined in broad terms."

The department also scanned the environment for promising growth areas such as energy and health care.   Once they had identified target areas, the NVD searched for "leads" or "hints" of technology which the company could incorporate into a venture.   For example, they had taken the energy area and "pretty well dissected it and determined what segments would be appropriate for U.S. Chemical."   An important part of this process of translating a business theme into specific products was communicating to the rest of the U.S Chemicals organization the areas which were of interest.

The search for technologies upon which projects could be based was aimed both internally and outside the company.   Nevertheless, all of the ventures launched by the NVD had been based on internally generated technologies.

A venture was typically aimed at a broadly defined market (such as health care) and consisted of a portfolio of several individual projects, each of which matched a company capability to a specific market need.

The survivors of this portfolio would lead the company into the desired new industry. For example, the manager of one venture explained that he was developing several product families simultaneously. These were parallel attempts to enter a broad industry. He saw his role as managing a portfolio, adding and deleting "leads" as he learned about the market.

As a general rule, the NVD did not want to get involved in small ventures which would not make a significant impact on company profits. One individual explained:

> "Our basic criterion is that we want a business with the future possibility of a noticeable impact on earnings per share."

Thus, individual projects (within a venture) were believed to have potential sales of $20 million or more within ten years.

The individual who headed up the search for venture opportunities explained further:

> "We are not interested in small business. We are looking for business themes to take to senior management for at least tentative approval. Then the task remains to translate these into specific product ideas."

A third individual in the NVD commented:

> "This company can't manage small businesses. A venture must have a potential of division size--$100-150 million in sales. It must have a business theme which can be speculated on and perceived as having large scale potential."

Venture Managers generally did not come from the ranks of researchers of "product champions." Most often they were staff members of the Development Projects department in the NVD who had worked on the venture in its earliest stages.

APPENDIX 3-2

LIFE-SPAN OF NVDs

Company	Year NVD Started	Year NVD Became Inoperative (-) Indicates NVD was Operating in 1975
1	Before 1960	-
2	1972	-
3	1967	1973
4	1973	-
5	1969	1975
6	1969	1971
7	1960	-
8	1973	-
9	1967	-
10	1970	1972
11	1967	-
12	1972	-
13	1974	1975
14	1969	1975
15	1968	1972
16	1968	1971
17	1968	1974
18	1973	-

APPENDIX 4-1
STANDARD CHEMICAL'S COMPANY FINANCIAL SUMMARY
1966-1975
($ MILLIONS)

	1975	1974	1973	1972	1971	1970	1969	1968	1967	1966
Net Sales and Operating Revenue	2119	2287	1732	1458	1272	1249	1170	1126	1005	991
Profit from Operations	115	255	243	209	157	163	147	162	135	151
Income Before Taxes on Income	61	216	236	191	141	146	130	152	133	157
Provision for Taxes on Income	12	78	99	88	63	67	60	69	60	73
Net Income	48	138	137	102	78	78	70	83	73	84
Capital Expenditures	226	325	216	119	79	136	96	168	196	104
Depreciation and Amortization	128	122	103	95	87	82	78	71	56	54
Long-Term Debt	501	523	266	189	195	269	279	323	239	90
Stockholders' Equity	997	984	894	797	724	674	638	609	563	524
Operating Assets	2807	2699	2179	1927	1710	1708	1627	1503	1320	1123

* Figures are disguised not to reveal identity of company, but ratios and trends have been kept approximately the same.

APPENDIX 5-1

DUPONT COMPANY
FINANCIAL AND OPERATING RECORD
1957-1966

Year	Sales	Average Operating Investment (a)	Construction Expenditures	Operating Income Net Amount	Operating Income Net As % of Average Operating Investment (a)	Total Net Income	Per Share of Common Stock Net Income DuPont Sources	Per Share of Common Stock Net Income General Motors Dividends (b)	Per Share of Common Stock Net Income Total	Cash Dividends Paid
		M I L L I O N S				(Million)				
1966	3,158	4,643	531	367	7 %	389	8.23	-	8.23	5.75
1965	2,999	4,267	326	384	9	407	8.63	-	8.63	6.00
1964	2,761	3,910	290	337	8	471	7.58	2.06	10.03	7.25
1963	2,554	3,604	370	310	8	472	6.84	3.21	10.05	7.75
1962	2,406	3,341	245	305	9	451	6.73	2.87	9.60	7.50
1961	2,191	3,120	204	258	8	418	5.72	3.16	8.88	7.50
1960	2,142	2,933	213	248	8	381	5.57	2.53	8.10	6.75
1959	2,114	2,745	174	288	10	418	6.38	2.54	8.92	7.00
1958	1,829	2,581	231	212	8	341	4.71	2.54	7.25	6.00
1957	1,964	2,421	220	265	11	396	5.93	2.55	8.48	6.50

(a) Operating Investment is the sum of "Total Current Assets" and "Plants and Properties" before deduction of accumulated depreciation and obsolescence, as shown in the company's consolidated balance sheets; the average is based on investment at the beginning and end of the year.

(b) In compliance with a U.S. District Court judgement, the company disposed of its entire investment of 63 million shares of General Motors Corporation common stock. Distributions made to holders of DuPont common stock in July 1962, January 1964, and January 1965, aggregated 1.36 shares of GM common stock for each share of DuPont common stock. In addition, 447,847 GM shares were sold in 1964.

APPENDIX 5-2

DUPONT COMPANY
FINANCIAL AND OPERATING RECORD
1967-1975

	1975(a)	1974(a)	1973	1972	1971	1970	1969	1968	1967
Sales	$ 7,222	$ 6,910	$ 5,964	$ 4,948	$ 4,371	$ 4,118	$ 4,133	$ 3,931	$ 3,519
Cost of goods and other operating charges	5,410	5,052	3,879	3,262	2,867	2,682	2,587	2,410	2,220
Interest expenses	126	62	35	24	18	18	15	11	10
Earnings before income taxes and minority interests	453	682	1,077	774	652	623	772	824	622
Income taxes	177	267	480	353	289	283	393	433	293
Earnings before minority interests	276	415	597	421	363	340	379	391	329
Percent of sales	3.8%	6.0%	10.0%	8.5%	8.3%	8.3%	9.2%	9.9%	9.3%
Percent return on average total investment (b)	2.5%	4.2%	6.8%	5.3%	4.9%	4.9%	5.8%	6.4%	5.7%
Net income	272	404	586	414	357	334	369	380	321
Net income earned on common stock	262	393	576	404	347	324	359	370	311
Per common share (c)	5.43	8.20	12.04	8.50	7.33	6.86	7.62	7.99	6.73
Percent return on average common stockholders' equity	7.4%	11.5%	18.0%	13.7%	12.4%	12.1%	14.1%	15.5%	13.7%
Dividends paid per common share	4.25	5.50	5.75	5.45	5.00	5.00	5.25	5.50	5.00
Dividends as % of amount earned on common stock	78%	67%	48%	64%	68%	73%	69%	69%	74%
Working capital	1,276	1,607	1,435	1,399	1,330	1,189	1,218	1,099	970
Plants & properties (d)	8,585	7,669	6,786	6,155	5,731	5,366	4,963	4,668	4,426
Total investments (b)	11,418	10,521	9,215	8,308	7,696	7,167	6,784	6,373	5,906
Long-term debt	889	793	250	241	236	162	147	114	99
Common stockholders' equity	3,596	3,514	3,355	3,029	2,856	2,725	2,615	2,458	2,319
For the year:									
Capital expenditures	1,066	1,038	781	561	474	499	417	355	466
Depreciation	580	506	450	418	399	372	351	324	302

(a)   DuPont adopted changes in 1974 and 1975.   See relevant annual reports for details.

(b)   Total investment is the sum of all assets as shown in the Company's consolidated balance sheets, before deduction of accumulated depreciation and obsolescence.

(c)   Based on the average number of common shares outstanding.

(d)   Before deduction of accumulated depreciation and obsolescence.

APPENDIX 6-1

RALSTON PURINA FINANCIAL SUMMARY
1958-1967

Fiscal Year Ended Sept. 30	Net Sales	Income Taxes		Net Earnings		Dividends Declared Common Stock	
1967	$1,275,211	$25,130	$ .83	$29,889	$ .99	$18,102	$ .60
1966	1,153,974	39,870	1.32	44,930	1.49	15,834	.53
1965	954,771	25,830	.86	29,540	.93	15,101	.50
1964	864,822	21,600	.71	24,350	.81	15,213	.50
1963	848,589	21,250	.70	23,324	.77	13,118	.43
1962	756,570	25,168	.83	25,238	.83	11,973	.40
1961	646,753	22,509	.75	22,859	.76	10,116	.34
1960	585,008	22,301	.75	21,122	.71	8,388	.28
1959	599,265	20,708	.70	20,013	.67	8,242	.28
1958	555,835	20,461	.69	18,808	.64	7,146	.24

Fiscal Year Ended Sept. 30	Capital Expenditures	Plant and Equipment	All Assets	Long-Term Debt	Common Shareholders Equity	Working Capital
1967	$50,988	$203,233	$549,322	$81,522	$274,566	$139,259
1966	37,512	174,901	481,774	67,345	261,360	142,563
1965	33,194	159,612	394,605	68,641	234,193	138,446
1964	17,329	145,429	364,484	65,824	220,680	136,080
1963	31,413	144,588	342,223	29,817	214,886	99,478
1962	29,503	124,228	315,791	33,184	203,922	102,035
1961	17,059	112,017	267,224	25,597	184,920	93,049
1960	18,253	104,175	249,178	27,118	170,939	89,793
1959	25,757	94,521	221,405	27,236	157,716	88,991
1958	11,777	75,660	220,836	29,097	145,239	96,310

APPENDIX 6-2

RALSTON PURINA FINANCIAL SUMMARY
1968-1975

(In millions except per share and percentage data)	1971	1970	1969	1968
Operating Results (for the year)				
Net Sales	$1,746	$1,567.0	$1,386.3	$1,281.5
Cost of Products Sold	1,425	1,262.1	1,126.6	1,056.4
Administrative, Research, Distribution and General Expenses	187	173.1	147.5	137.9
Interest Expense	21	15.6	13.5	13.2
Income Taxes	54	59.4	51.8	36.8
Earnings for the Year	55	56.8	46.9	37.2
As a Percent of Sales	3.2%	3.6%	3.4%	2.9%
Earnings Per Common Share				
Primary	$ 1.72	$ 1.78	$ 1.47	$ 1.16
Fully Diluted	1.63	1.67	1.39	1.12
Return on Average Shareholders Equity	14.3%	15.9%	14.5%	12.6%
Common Share Outstanding (average)	31.7	31.0	30.7	30.4
Dividends Declared on Common Stock	$ 22.1	$ 20.9	$ 18.5	$ 18.3
Per Share	.70	.68	.60	.60
Financial Position (at year end)				
Working Capital	$ 240	$ 170.3	$ 175.3	$ 175.6
Plant and Equipment	411	362.1	305.1	257.9
Additions and Replacements (during year)	92	95.1	83.2	61.2
Depreciation (during year)	29	28.3	24.0	22.2
Total Assets	897	775.2	676.2	626.9
Long-term Debt	264	178.9	162.1	140.3
Shareholders Equity	403	373.8	338.3	307.0
Per Common Share	11.47	10.39	9.18	8.19
Common Shares Outstanding	32	31.2	30.9	30.6
Market Price Range of Common Stock	35-21½	30 5/8-19½	28½-21 1/3	27 3/4-20½

Appendix 6-2
(cont.)

(In millions except per share and percentage data)	1975	1974	1973	1972
Operating Results (for the year				
Net Sales	$3,149.1	$3,073.2	$2,433.6	$1,833.4
Cost of Products Sold	2,596.8	2,581.2	2,019.3	1,480.1
Administrative, Research, Distribution and General Expenses	328.6	266.2	242.5	211.5
Interest Expense	36.7	33.8	25.0	21.6
Income Taxes	87.5	81.3	69.2	57.5
Earnings for the Year	99.5	90.7	77.6	62.7
As a Percent of Sales	3.2%	3.0%	3.2%	3.4%
Earnings Per Common Share				
Primary	$ 2.80	$ 2.56	$ 2.22	$ 1.87
Fully Diluted	2.75	2.56	2.19	1.79
Return on Average Shareholders Equity	15.6%	15.9%	15.2%	14.1%
Common Shares Outstanding (average)	35.6	35.4	34.8	33.2
Dividends Declared on Common Stock	$ 32.0	$ 28.3	$ 26.3	$ 23.6
Per Share	.90	.80	.75	.70
Financial Position (at year end)				
Working Capital	$ 406.6	$ 304.4	$ 338.9	$ 232.8
Plant and Equipment	654.9	586.7	490.7	438.9
Additions and Replacements (during year)	133.4	149.0	108.0	80.5
Depreciation (during year)	48.0	40.4	35.0	32.5
Total Assets	1,377.3	1,349.7	1,133.4	933.0
Long-Term Debt	392.6	305.9	304.1	208.7
Shareholders Equity	674.3	602.6	537.4	484.0
Per Common Share	18.91	16.93	15.20	13.49
Common Shares Outstanding	35.7	35.5	35.4	34.4
Market Price Range of Common Stock	45¼ - 30 5/8	49 3/4- 29	45½ -32½	43-31

APPENDIX 6-3

RALSTON PURINA COMPANY CORPORATE OBJECTIVES

Ralston Purina Company

CORPORATE OBJECTIVES

Our primary objective is to optimize use of our resources . . . to produce short- and long-term profit growth consistent with the balanced best interest of customers, shareholders, employees, suppliers, and society at large. To achieve these results, we must perform effectively in the following key result areas:

> Customer satisfaction . . . Management development and performance . . . Employee attitude and performance . . . Social responsibility . . . Productivity . . . Innovation.

1

We recognize that the primary purpose of our business is to perform a necessary economic service by creating, stimulating, and satisfying customers. We must be a market-oriented company dedicated to the principle that, in order to supply the right product or service at the right time and in the right way, we need first to establish what the customer wants, where, when, how, and at what price.

2

Building on our base of protein and nutrition, we will remain diversified in our operations, multinational in organization, and global in outlook.

3

We dedicate ourselves to the principle of continuous self-renewal so that individuals, organization structure, products, facilities, and systems do not stagnate. We recognize that:

- People are the ultimate source of renewal. We will bring to the corporation a steady flow of able and highly motivated individuals and then provide positive, constructive programs of management development.
- Organizational structure must be flexible. We will evolve subject only to the yardstick of what is most successful and meets our requirements.
- We will continue to ask the question "What Next?" We must recognize and manage the accelerating rate of change.
- We will analyze assets and functions in which potential is diminishing in terms of contribution to earnings, cash flow, and tie-in value to other units in order to develop a course of action which may include disinvestment.

- We must maintain an environment which fosters individual effort, rewards initiative and encourages the free and open exchange of ideas; self-criticism and constant restudy are vital to the present health of the enterprise and are essential elements to future growth—we welcome challenging positions and opinions.
- We will maintain effective and simple systems and procedures to implement organizational structure, and we will evaluate them at regular intervals.
- Since the dynamics of an organization are related to motivation, conviction and morale, we will endeavor to make every employee know that his optimum efforts make a difference.
- We must be results-oriented, measured and held responsible.

- We must create a climate of technology, special knowledges, and services which induce in our customers a desire to buy our products and/or our services.

4

We will consistently and systematically strive to delegate decision-making authority intelligently to the proper lowest level without abrogating management responsibilities. We will measure qualitative and quantitative results through a simple and sensitive control system.

Author's Note: Ralston Purina Company does not designate the Venture Management areas, which is the subject of this case study as a "line of business" or "operating group" for purposes of its financial statements. Accordingly, the financial information contained herein consists in some measure of hypotheses, postulations and derivations from the Company's published financial statements. While the content of this case study was discussed with Company officials, and is believed to be a valid overall view of the Venture Management area, Company officials have expressed no view as to the accuracy of most of the specific financial information contained herein.

INDEX